Imperial Purple

Edgar Saltus

Contents

IMPERIAL PURPLE

BY

Edgar Saltus

I
THAT WOMAN

When the murder was done and the heralds shouted through the thick streets the passing of Caesar, it was the passing of the republic they announced, the foundation of Imperial Rome. There was a hush, then a riot which frightened a senate that frightened the world. Caesar was adored. A man who could give millions away and sup on dry bread was apt to conquer, not provinces alone, but hearts. Besides, he had begun well and his people had done their best. The House of Julia, to which he belonged, descended, he declared, from Venus. The ancestry was less legendary than typical. Cinna drafted a law giving him the right to marry as often as he chose. His mistresses were queens. After the episodes in Gaul, when he entered Rome his legions warned the citizens to have an eye on their wives. At seventeen he fascinated pirates. A shipload of the latter had caught him and demanded twenty talents ransom. "Too little," said the lad; "I will give you fifty, and impale you too," which he did, jesting with them meanwhile, reciting verses of his own composition, calling them barbarians when they did not applaud, ordering them to be quiet when he wished to sleep, captivating them by the effrontery of his assurance, and, the ransom paid, slaughtering them as he had promised.

Tall, slender, not handsome, but superb and therewith so perfectly sent out that Cicero mistook him for a fop from whom the republic had nothing to fear; splendidly lavish, exquisitely gracious, he was born to charm, and his charm was such that it still subsists. Cato alone was unenthralled. But Cato was never pleased; he laughed but once, and all Rome turned out to see him; he belonged to an earlier day, to an austerer, perhaps to a better one, and it may be that in "that woman," as he called Caesar, his clearer vision discerned beneath the plumage of the peacock, the beak and talons of the bird of prey. For they were there, and needed only a vote of the senate to batten on nations of which the senate had never heard. Loan him an army, and "that woman" was to give geography such a twist that today whoso says Caesar says history.

Was it this that Cato saw, or may it be that one of the oracles which had not ceased to speak had told him of that coming night when he was to take his own life, fearful lest "that woman" should overwhelm him with the magnificence of his forgiveness? Cato walks through history, as he walked through the Forum, bare of foot--too severe to be simple, too obstinate to be generous--the image of ancient Rome.

In Caesar there was nothing of this. He was wholly modern; dissolute enough for any epoch, but possessed of virtues that his contemporaries could not spell. A slave tried to poison him. Suetonius says he merely put the slave to death. The "merely" is to the point. Cato would have tortured him first. After Pharsalus he forgave everyone. When severe, it was to himself. It is true he turned over two million people into so many dead flies, their legs in the air, creating, as Tacitus has it, a solitude which he described as Peace; but what antitheses may not be expected in a man who, before the first century was begun, divined the fifth, and who in the Suevians--that terrible people beside whom no nation could live--foresaw Attila!

Save in battle his health was poor. He was epileptic, his strength undermined by incessant debauches; yet let a nation fancying him months away put on insurgent airs, and on that nation he descended as the thunder does. In his campaigns time and again he overtook his own messengers. A phantom in a ballad was not swifter than he. Simultaneously his sword flashed in Germany, on the banks of the Adriatic, in that Ultima Thule where the Britons lived. From the depths of Gaul he dominated Rome, and therewith he was penetrating impenetrable forests, trailing legions as a torch trails smoke, erecting walls that a nation could not cross, turning soldiers into marines, infantry into cavalry, building roads that are roads to-day, fighting with one hand and writing an epic with the other, dictating love-letters, chronicles, dramas; finding time to make a collection of witticisms; overturning thrones while he decorated Greece; mingling initiate into orgies of the Druids, and, as the cymbals clashed, coquetting with those terrible virgins who awoke the tempest; not only conquering, but captivating, transforming barbarians into soldiers and those soldiers into senators, submitting three hundred nations and ransacking Britannia for pearls for his mistresses' ears.

Each epoch has its secret, and each epoch-maker his own. Caesar's secret lay in the power he had of projecting a soul into the ranks of an army, of making legions and their leader one. Disobedience only he punished; anything else he forgave. After a victory his soldiery did what they liked. He gave them arms, slaves to burnish them, women, feasts, sleep. They were his comrades; he called them so; he wept at the death of any of them, and when they were frightened, as they were in Gaul before they met the Germans, and in Africa before they encountered Juba, Caesar frightened them still more. He permitted no questions, no making of wills. The cowards could hide where they liked; his old guard, the Tenth, would do the work alone; or, threat still more sinister, he would command a retreat. Ah, that, never! Fanaticism returned, the legions begged to be punished.

Michelet says he would like to have seen him crossing Gaul, bareheaded, in the rain. It would have been as interesting, perhaps, to have watched him beneath the shade of the velarium pleading the cause of Masintha against the Numidian king. Before him was a crowd that covered not the Forum alone, but the steps of the adjacent temples, the roofs of the basilicas, the arches of Janus, one that extended remotely to the black walls of the Curia Hostilia beyond. And there, on the rostrum, a musician behind him supplying the la from a flute, the air filled with gold motes, Caesar, his toga becomingly adjusted, a jewelled hand extended, opened for the defence. Presently, when through the exercise of that art of his which Cicero pronounced incomparable, he felt that the sympathy of the audience was won, it would have been interesting, indeed, to have heard him argue point after point-- clearly, brilliantly, wittily; insulting the plaintiff in poetic terms; consigning him gracefully to the infernal regions; accentuating a fictitious and harmonious anger; drying his forehead without disarranging his hair; suffocating with the emotions he evoked; displaying real tears, and with them a knowledge, not only of law, rhetoric, philosophy, but of geometry, astronomy, ethics and the fine arts; blinding his hearers with the coruscations of his erudition; stirring them with his tongue, as with the point of a sword, until, as though abruptly possessed by an access of fury, he seized the plaintiff by the beard and sent him spinning like a leaf which the wind had caught.

It would have bored no one either to have assisted at his triumph when he returned from Gaul, when he returned after Spain, after Pharsalus, when he returned from Cleopatra's arms.

On that day the Via Sacra was curtained with silk. To the blare of twisted bugles there descended to it from the turning at the hill a troop of musicians garmented in leather tunics, bonneted with lions' heads. Behind them a hundred bulls, too fat to be troublesome, and decked for death, bellowed musingly at the sacrifants, who, naked to the waist, a long-handled hammer on the shoulder, maintained them with colored cords. To the rumble of wide wheels and the thunder of spectators the prodigious booty passed, and with it triumphs of war, vistas of conquered countries, pictures of battles, lists of the vanquished, symbols of cities that no longer were; a stretch of ivory on which shone three words, each beginning with a V; images of gods disturbed, the Rhine, the Rhone, the captive Ocean in massive gold; the glitter of three thousand crowns offered to the dictator by the army and allies of Rome. Then came the standards of the republic, a swarm of eagles, the size of pigeons, in polished silver upheld by lances which ensigns bore, preceding the six hundred senators who marched in a body, their togas bordered with red, while to the din of incessant insults, interminable files of prisoners passed, their wrists chained to iron collars, which held their heads very straight, and to the rear a litter, in which crouched the Vercingetorix of Gaul, a great moody giant, his menacing eyes nearly hidden in the tangles of his tawny hair.

When they had gone the street was alive with explosions of brass, aflame with the burning red cloaks of laureled lictors making way for the coming of Caesar. Four horses, harnessed abreast, their manes dyed, their forelocks puffed, drew a high and wonderfully jewelled car; and there, in the attributes and attitude of Jupiter Capitolinus, Caesar sat, blinking his tired eyes. His face and arms were painted vermilion; above the Tyrian purple of his toga, above the gold work and palms of his tunic, there oscillated a little ball in which there were charms against Envy. On his head a wreath concealed his increasing baldness; along his left arm the sceptre lay; behind him a boy admonished him noisily to remember he was man, while to the rear for miles and miles there rang the laugh of trumpets, the click of castanets, the shouts of dancers, the roar of the multitude, the tramp of legions, and the cry, caught up and repeated, "Io! Triomphe!"

Presently, in the temple of the god of gods, side by side with the statue of Jupiter, Caesar found his own statue with "Caesar, demi-god," at its base. The captive chiefs disappeared in the Tullianum, and a herald called, "They have lived!" Through the squares jesters circulated, polyglot and obscene; across the Tiber, in an artificial lake, the flotilla of Egypt fought against that of Tyr; in the amphitheatre there was a combat of soldiers, infantry against cavalry, one that indemnified those that had not seen the massacres in Thessaly and in Spain. There were public feasts, gifts to everyone. Tables were set in the Forum, in the circuses and theatres. Falernian circulated in amphorae, Chios in barrels. When the populace was gorged there were the red feathers to enable it to gorge again. Of the Rome of Romulus there was nothing left save the gaunt she-wolf, her wide lips curled at the descendants of her nursling.

Later, when in slippered feet Caesar wandered through those lovely gardens of his that lay beyond the Tiber, it may be that he recalled a dream which had come to him as a lad; one which concerned the submission of his mother; one which had disturbed him until the sooth-sayers said: "The mother you saw is the earth, and you will be her master." And as the memory of the dream returned, perhaps with it came the memory of the hour when as simple quaestor he had wept at Gaddir before a statue that was there. Demi-god, yes; he was that. More, even; he was dictator, but the dream was unfulfilled. There were the depths of Hither Asia, the mysteries that lay beyond; there were the glimmering plains of the Caucasus; there were the Vistula and the Baltic; the diadems of Cyrus and of Alexander defying his ambition yet, and what were triumphs and divinity to one who would own the world!

It was this that preoccupied him. The immensity of his successes seemed petty and Rome very small. Heretofore he had forgiven those who had opposed him. Presently his attitude changed, and so subtly that it was the more humiliating; it was not that he no longer forgave, he disdained to punish. His contempt was absolute. The senate made his office of pontifix maximus hereditary and accorded the title of Imperator to his heirs. He snubbed the senate and the honors that it brought. The senate was shocked. Composed of men whose fortunes he had made, the senate was not only shocked, its education in ingratitude was complete. Already there had been murmurs. Not content with disarranging the calendar, outlining an empire, drafting a code while planning fresh beauties, new theatres, bilingual libraries, larger temples, grander gods, Caesar was at work in the markets, in the kitchens of the gourmets, in the jewel-boxes of the virgins. Liberty, visibly, was taking flight. Besides, the power concentrated in him might be so pleasantly distributed. It was decided that Caesar was in the way. To put him out of it a pretext was necessary.

One day the senate assembled at his command. They were to sign a decree creating him king. In order not to, Suetonius says, they killed him, wounding each other in the effort, for Caesar fought like the demon that he was, desisting only when he recognized Brutus, to whom, in Greek, he muttered a reproach, and, draping his toga that he might fall with decency, sank backward, his head covered, a few feet from the bronze wolf that stood, its ears pointed at the letters S. P. Q. R. which decorated a frieze of the Curia.

Brutus turned to harangue the senate; it had fled. He went to the Forum to address the people; there was no one. Rome was strangely empty. Doors were barricaded, windows closed. Through the silent streets gladiators prowled. Night came, and with it whispering groups. The groups thickened, voices mounted. Caesar's will had been read. He had left his gardens to the people, a gift to every citizen, his wealth and power to his butchers. The body, which two slaves had removed, an arm hanging from the litter, had never been as powerfully alive. Caesar reigned then as never before. A mummer mouthed:

"I brought them life, they gave me death."

And willingly would the mob have made Rome the funeral pyre of their idol. In the sky a comet appeared. It was his soul on its way to Olympus.

II
CONJECTURAL ROME

"I received Rome in brick; I shall leave it in marble," said Augustus, who was fond of fine phrases, a trick he had caught from Vergil. And when he looked from his home on the Palatine over the glitter of the Forum and the glare of the Capitol to the new and wonderful precinct which extended to the Field of Mars, there was a stretch of splendor which sanctioned the boast. The city then was very vast. The tourist might walk in it, as in the London of to-day, mile after mile, and at whatever point he placed himself, Rome still lay beyond; a Rome quite like London--one that was choked with mystery, with gold and curious crime.

But it was not all marble. There were green terraces and porphyry porticoes that leaned to a river on which red galleys passed; there were theatres in which a multitude could jeer at an emperor, and arenas in which an emperor could watch a multitude die; there were bronze doors and garden roofs, glancing villas and temples that defied the sun; there were spacious streets, a Forum curtained with silk, the glint and evocations of triumphal war, the splendor of a host of gods, but it was not all marble; there were rents in the magnificence and tatters in the laticlave of state.

In the Subura, where at night women sat in high chairs, ogling the passer with painted eyes, there was still plenty of brick; tall tenements, soiled linen, the odor of Whitechapel and St. Giles. The streets were noisy with match-peddlers, with vendors of cake and tripe and coke; there were touts there too, altars to unimportant divinities, lying Jews who dealt in old clothes, in obscene pictures and unmentionable wares; at the crossings there were thimbleriggers, clowns and jugglers, who made glass balls appear and disappear surprisingly; there were doorways decorated with curious invitations, gossipy barber shops, where, through the liberality of politicians, the scum of a great city was shaved, curled and painted free; and there were public houses, where vagabond slaves and sexless priests drank the mulled wine of Crete, supped on the flesh of beasts slaughtered in the arena, or watched the Syrian women twist to the click of castanets.

Beyond were gray quadrangular buildings, the stomach of Rome, through which, each noon, ediles passed, verifying the prices, the weights and measures of the market men, examining the fish and meats, the enormous cauliflowers that came from the suburbs, Veronese carrots, Arician pears, stout thrushes, suckling pigs, eggs embedded in grass, oysters from Baiae, boxes of onions and garlic mixed, mountains of poppies, beans and fennel, destroying whatever had ceased to be fresh and taxing that which was.

On the Via Sacra were the shops frequented by ladies; bazaars where silks and xylons were to be had, essences and unguents, travelling boxes of scented wood, switches of yellow hair, useful drugs such as hemlock, aconite, mandragora and cantharides; the last thing of Ovid's and the improper little novels that came from Greece.

On the Appian Way, through green afternoons and pink arcades, fashion strolled. There wealth passed in its chariots, smart young men that smelt of cinnamon instead of war, nobles, matrons, cocottes.

At the other end of the city, beyond the menagerie of the Pantheon, was the Field of Mars, an open-air gymnasium, where every form of exercise was to be had, even to that simple promenade in which the Romans delighted, and which in Caesar's camp so astonished the Verronians that they thought the promenaders crazy and offered to lead them to their tents. There was tennis for those who liked it; racquets, polo, football, quoits, wrestling, everything apt to induce perspiration and prepare for the hour when a gong of bronze announced the opening of the baths--those wonderful baths, where the Roman, his slaves about him, after passing through steam and water and the hands of the masseur, had every hair plucked from his arms, legs and armpits; his flesh rubbed down with nard, his limbs polished with pumice; and then, wrapped in a scarlet robe, lined with fur, was sent home in a litter. "Strike them in the face!" cried Caesar at Pharsalus, when the young patricians made their charge; and the young patricians, who cared more for their looks than they did for victory, turned and fled.

It was to the Field of Mars that Agrippa came, to whom Rome owed the Pantheon and the demand for a law which should inhibit the private ownership of a masterpiece. There, too, his eunuchs about him, Mecaenas lounged, companioned by Varus, by Horace and the mime Bathylle, all of whom he was accustomed to invite to that lovely villa of his which overlooked the blue Sabinian hills, and where suppers were given such as those which Petronius has described so alertly and so well.

In the hall like that of Mecaenas', one divided against itself, the upper half containing the couches and tables, the other reserved for the service and the entertainments that follow, the ceiling was met by columns, the walls hidden by panels of gems. On a frieze twelve pictures, surmounted by the signs of the zodiac, represented the dishes of the different months. Beneath the bronze beds and silver tables mosaics were set in imitation of food that had fallen and had not been swept away. And there, in white ungirdled tunics, the head and neck circled with coils of amaranth--the perfume of which in opening the pores neutralizes the fumes of wine--the guests lay, fanned by boys, whose curly hair they used for napkins. Under the supervision of butlers the courses were served on platters so large that they covered the tables; sows' breasts with Lybian truffles; dormice baked in poppies and honey, peacock-tongues flavored with cinnamon; oysters stewed in garum--a sauce made of the intestines of fish--sea-wolves from the Baltic; sturgeons from Rhodes; fig-peckers from Samos; African snails; pale beans in pink lard; and a yellow pig cooked after the Troan fashion, from which, when carved, hot sausages fell and live thrushes flew. Therewith was the mulsum, a cup made of white wine, nard, roses, absinthe and honey; the delicate sweet wines of Greece; and crusty Falernian of the year six hundred and thirty-two. As the cups circulated, choirs entered, chanting sedately the last erotic song; a clown danced on the top of a ladder, which he maintained upright as he danced, telling meanwhile untellable stories to the frieze; and host and guests, unvociferously, as good breeding dictates, chatted through the pauses of the service; discussed the disadvantages of death, the value of Noevian iambics, the disgrace of Ovid, banished because of Livia's eyes.

Such was the Rome of Augustus. "Caesar," cried a mime to him one day, "do you know that it is important for you that the people should be interested in Bathylle and in myself?"

The mime was right. The sovereign of Rome was not the Caesar, nor yet the aristocracy. The latter was dead. It had been banished by barbarian senators, by barbarian gods; it had died twice, at Pharsalus, at Philippi; it was the people that was sovereign, and it was important that that sovereign should be amused--flattered, too, and fed. For thirty years not a Roman of note had died in his bed; not one but had kept by him a slave who should kill him when his hour had come; anarchy had been continuous; but now Rome was at rest and its sovereign wished to laugh. Made up of every nation and every vice, the universe was ransacked for its entertainment. The mountain sent its lions, the desert giraffes; there were boas from the jungles, bulls from the plains, and hippopotami from the waters of the Nile. Into the arenas patricians descended; in the amphitheatre there were criminals from Gaul; in the Forum philosophers from Greece. On the stage, there were tragedies, pantomimes and farce; there were races in the circus, and in the sacred groves girls with the

Orient in their eyes and slim waists that swayed to the crotals. For the thirst of the sovereign there were aqueducts, and for its hunger Africa, Egypt, Sicily contributed grain. Syria unveiled her altars, Persia the mystery and magnificence of her gods.

Such was Rome. Augustus was less noteworthy; so unnecessary even that every student must regret Actium, Antony's defeat, the passing of Caesar's dream. For Antony was made for conquests; it was he who, fortune favoring, might have given the world to Rome. A splendid, an impudent bandit, first and foremost a soldier, calling himself a descendant of Hercules whom he resembled; hailed at Ephesus as Bacchus, in Egypt as Osiris; Asiatic in lavishness, and Teuton in his capacity for drink; vomiting in the open Forum, and making and unmaking kings; weaving with that viper of the Nile a romance which is history; passing initiate into the inimitable life, it would have been curious to have watched him that last night when the silence was stirred by the hum of harps, the cries of bacchantes bearing his tutelary god back to the Roman camp, while he said farewell to love, to empire and to life.

Augustus resembled him not at all. He was a colorless monarch; an emperor in everything but dignity, a prince in everything but grace; a tactician, not a soldier; a superstitious braggart, afraid of nothing but danger; seducing women to learn their husband's secrets; exiling his daughter, not because she had lovers, but because she had other lovers than himself; exiling Ovid because of Livia, who in the end poisoned her prince, and adroitly, too; illiterate, blundering of speech, and coarse of manner--a hypocrite and a comedian in one--so guileful and yet so stupid that while a credulous moribund ordered the gods to be thanked that Augustus survived him, the people publicly applied to him an epithet which does not look well in print.

After Philippi and the suicide of Brutus; after Actium and Antony's death, for the first time in ages, the gates of the Temple of Janus were closed. There was peace in the world; but it was the sword of Caesar, not of Augustus, that brought the insurgents to book. At each of the victories he was either asleep or ill. At the time of battle there was always some god warning him to be careful. The battle won, he was brave enough, considerate even. A father and son begged for mercy. He promised forgiveness to the son on condition that he killed his father. The son accepted and did the work; then he had the son despatched. A prisoner begged but for a grave. "The vultures will see to it," he answered. When at the head of Caesar's legions, he entered Rome to avenge the latter's death, he announced beforehand that he would imitate neither Caesar's moderation nor Sylla's cruelty. There would be only a few proscriptions, and a price--and what a price, liberty!--was placed on the heads of hundreds of senators and thousands of knights. And these people, who had more slaves than they knew by sight, slaves whom they tossed alive to fatten fish, slaves to whom they affected never to speak, and who were crucified did they so much as sneeze in their presence--at the feet of these slaves they rolled, imploring them not to deliver them up. Now and then a slave was merciful; Augustus never.

Successes such as these made him ambitious. Having vanquished with the sword, he tried the pen. "You may grant the freedom of the city to your barbarians," said a wit to him one day, "but not to your solecisms." Undeterred he began a tragedy entitled "Ajax," and discovering his incompetence, gave it up. "And what has become of Ajax?" a parasite asked. "Ajax threw himself on a sponge," replied Augustus, whose father, it is to be regretted, did not do likewise. Nevertheless, it were pleasant to have assisted at his funeral.

A couch of ivory and gold, ten feet high, draped with purple, stood for a week in the atrium of the palace. Within the couch, hidden from view, the body of the emperor lay, ravaged by poison. Above was a statue, recumbent, in wax, made after his image and dressed in imperial robes. Near by a little slave with a big fan protected the statue from flies. Each day physicians came, gazed at the closed wax mouth, and murmured, "He is worse." In the vestibule was a pot of burning ilex, and stretching out through the portals a branch of cypress warned the pontiffs from the contamination of the sight of death.

At high noon on the seventh day the funeral crossed the city. First were the flaming torches; the statues of the House of Octavia; senators in blue; knights in scarlet; magistrates; lictors; the pick of the praetorian guard. Then, to the alternating choruses of boys and girls, the rotting body passed down the Sacred Way. Behind it Tiberius in a travelling-cloak, his hands unringed, marched meditating on the curiosities of life, while to the rear there straggled a troop of dancing satyrs, led by a mime dressed in resemblance of Augustus, whose defects he caricatured, whose vices he parodied and on whom the surging crowd closed in.

On the Field of Mars the pyre had been erected, a great square structure of resinous wood, the interior filled with coke and sawdust, the exterior covered with illuminated cloths, on which, for base, a tower rose, three storeys high. Into the first storey flowers and perfumes were thrown, into the second the couch was raised, then a torch was applied.

As the smoke ascended an eagle shot from the summit, circled a moment, and disappeared. For the sum of a million sesterces a senator swore that with the eagle he had seen the emperor's soul.

III
FABULOUS FIELDS

Mention Tiberius, and the name evokes a taciturn tyrant, devising in the crypts of a palace infamies so monstrous that to describe them new words were coined.

In the Borghese collection Tiberius is rather good-looking than otherwise, not an Antinous certainly, but manifestly a dreamer; one whose eyes must have been almost feline in their abstraction, and in the corners of whose mouth you detect pride, no doubt, but melancholy as well. The pride was congenital, the melancholy was not.

Under Tiberius there was quiet, a romancer wrote, and the phrase in its significance passed into legend. During the dozen or more years that he ruled in Rome, his common sense was obvious. The Tiber overflowed, the senate looked for a remedy in the Sibyline Books. Tiberius set some engineers to work. A citizen swore by Augustus and swore falsely. The senate sought to punish him, not for perjury but for sacrilege. It is for Augustus to punish, said Tiberius. The senate wanted to name a month after him. Tiberius declined. "Supposing I were the thirteenth Caesar, what would you do?" For years he reigned, popular and acclaimed, caring the while nothing for popularity and less for pomp. Sagacious, witty even, believing perhaps in little else than fate and mathematics, yet maintaining the institutions of the land, striving resolutely for the best, outwardly impassable and inwardly mobile, he was a man and his patience had bounds. There were conspirators in the atrium, there was death in the courtier's smile; and finding his favorites false, his life threatened, danger at every turn, his conception of rulership changed. Where moderation had been suddenly there gleamed the axe.

Tacitus, always dramatic, states that at the time terror devastated the city. It so happened that under the republic there was a law against whomso diminished the majesty of the people. The republic was a god, one that had its temple, its priests, its altars. When the republic succumbed, its divinity passed to the emperor; he became Jupiter's peer, and, as such, possessed of a majesty which it was sacrilege to slight. Consulted on the subject, Tiberius replied that the law must be observed. Originally instituted in prevention of offences against the public good, it was found to change into a crime, a word, a gesture or a look. It was a crime to undress before a statue of Augustus, to mention his name in the latrinae, to carry a coin with his image into a lupanar. The punishment was death. Of the property of the accused, a third went to the informer, the rest to the state. Then abruptly terror stalked abroad. No one was safe except the obscure, and it was the obscure that accused. Once an accused accused his accuser; the latter went mad. There was but one refuge--the tomb. If the accused had time to kill himself before he was tried, his property was safe from seizure and his corpse from disgrace. Suicide became endemic in Rome. Never among the rich were orgies as frenetic as then. There was a breathless chase after delights, which the summons, "It is time to die," might at any moment interrupt.

Tiberius meanwhile had gone from Rome. It was then his legend began. He was represented living at Capri in a collection of twelve villas, each of which was dedicated to a particular form of lust, and there with the paintings of Parrhasius for stimulant the satyr lounged. He was then an old man; his life had been passed in public, his conduct unreproved. If no one becomes suddenly base, it is rare for a man of seventy to become abruptly vile. "Whoso," Sakya Muni announced--"whoso discovers that grief comes from affection, will retire into the jungles and there remain." Tiberius had made the discovery. The jungles he selected were the gardens by the sea. And in those gardens, gossip represented him devising new forms of old vice. On the subject every doubt is permissible, and even otherwise, morality then existed in but one form, one which the entire nation observed, wholly, absolutely; that form was patriotism. Chastity was expected of the vestal, but of no one else. The matrons had certain traditions to maintain, certain appearances to preserve, but otherwise morality was unimagined and matrimony unpopular.

When matrimony occurred, divorce was its natural consequence. Incompatibility was sufficient cause. Cicero, who has given it to history that the best women counted the years not numerically, but by their different husbands, obtained a divorce on the ground that his wife did not idolize him.

Divorce was not obligatory. Matrimony was. According to a recent law whoso at twenty-five was not married, whoso, divorced or widowed, did not remarry, whoso, though married, was without children, was regarded as a public enemy and declared incapable of inheriting or of serving the state. To this law, one of Augustus' stupidities which presently fell into disuse, only a technical observance was paid. Men married just enough to gain a position or inherit a legacy; next day they got a divorce. At the moment of need a child was adopted; the moment passed, the child was disowned. But if the law had little value, at least it shows the condition of things. Moreover, if in that condition Tiberius participated, it was not because he did not differ from other men.

"Ho sempre amato la solitaria vita," Petrarch, referring to himself, declared, and Tiberius might have said the same thing. He was in love with solitude; ill with efforts for the unattained; sick with the ingratitude of man. Presently it was decided that he had lived long enough. He was suffocated--beneath a mattress at that. Caesar had dreamed of a universal monarchy of which he should be king; he was murdered. That dream was also Antony's; he killed himself. Cato had sought the restoration of the republic, and Brutus the attainment of virtue; both committed suicide. Under the empire dreamers fared ill. Tiberius was a dreamer.

In a palace where a curious conception of the love of Atalanta and Meleager was said to figure on the walls, there was a door on which was a sign, imitated from one that overhung the Theban library of Osymandias--Pharmacy of the Soul. It was there Tiberius dreamed.

On the ivory shelves were the philtres of Parthenius, labelled De Amatoriis Affectionibus, the Sybaris of Clitonymus, the Erotopaegnia of Laevius, the maxims and instructions of Elephantis, the nine books of Sappho. There also were the pathetic adventures of Odatis and Zariadres, which Chares of Mitylene had given to the world; the astonishing tales of that early Cinderella, Rhodopis; and with them those romances of Ionian nights by Aristides of Milet, which Crassus took with him when he set out to subdue the Parthians, and which; found in the booty, were read aloud to the people that they might judge the morals of a nation that pretended to rule the world.

Whether such medicaments are serviceable to the soul is problematic. Tiberius had other drugs on the ivory shelves--magic preparations that transported him to fabulous fields. There was a work by Hecataesus, with which he could visit Hyperborea, that land where happiness was a birthright, inalienable at that; yet a happiness so sweet that it must have been cloying; for the people who enjoyed it, and with it the appanage of limitless life, killed themselves from sheer ennui. Theopompus disclosed to him a stranger vista--a continent beyond the ocean--one where there were immense cities, and where two rivers flowed--the River of Pleasure and the River of Pain. With Iambulus he discovered the Fortunate Isles, where there were men with elastic bones, bifurcated tongues; men who never married, who worshipped the sun, whose life was an uninterrupted delight, and who, when overtaken by age, lay on a perfumed grass that produced a voluptuous death. Evhemerus, a terrible atheist, whose Sacred History the early bishops wielded against polytheism until they discovered it was double-edged, took him to Panchaia, an island where incense grew; where property was held in common; where there was but one law--Justice, yet a justice different from our own, one which Hugo must have intercepted when he made an entrancing yet enigmatical apparition exclaim:

"Tu me crois la Justice, je suis la Pitie."

And in this paradise there was a temple, and before it a column, about which, in Panchaian characters, ran a history of ancient kings, who, to the astonishment of the tourist, were found to be none other than the gods whom the universe worshipped, and who in earlier days had announced themselves divinities, the better to rule the hearts and minds of man.

With other guides Tiberius journeyed through lands where dreams come true. Aristeas of Proconnesus led him among the Arimaspi, a curious people who passed their lives fighting for gold with griffons in the dark. With Isogonus he descended the valley of Ismaus, where wild men were, whose feet turned inwards. In Albania he found a race with pink eyes and white hair; in Sarmatia another that ate only on alternate days. Agatharcides took him to Libya, and there introduced him to the Psyllians, in whose bodies was a poison deadly to serpents, and who, to test the fidelity of their wives, placed their children in the presence of snakes; if the snakes fled they knew their wives were pure. Callias took him further yet, to the home of the hermaphrodites; Nymphodorus showed him a race of fascinators who used enchanted words. With Apollonides he encountered women who killed with their eyes those on whom they looked too long. Megasthenes guided him to the Astomians, whose garments were the down of feathers, and who lived on the scent of the rose.

In his cups they all passed, confusedly, before him; the hermaphrodites whispered to the rose-breathers the secrets of impossible love; the griffons bore to him women with magical eyes; the Albanians danced with elastic feet; he heard the shrill call of the Psyllians, luring the serpents to death; the column of Panchaia unveiled its mysteries; the Hyperboreans the reason of their fear of life, and on the wings of the chimera he set out again in search of that continent which haunted antiquity and which lay beyond the sea.

IV
THE PURSUIT OF THE IMPOSSIBLE

"Another Phaethon for the universe," Tiberius is reported to have muttered, as he gazed at his nephew Caius, nicknamed Caligula, who was to suffocate him with a mattress and rule in his stead.

To rule is hardly the expression. There is no term in English to convey that dominion over sea and sky which a Caesar possessed, and which Caligula was the earliest to understand. Augustus was the first magistrate of Rome, Tiberius the first citizen. Caligula was the first emperor, but an emperor hallucinated by the enigma of his own grandeur, a prince for whose sovereignty the world was too small.

Each epoch has its secret, sometimes puerile, often perplexing; but in its maker there is another and a more interesting one yet. Eliminate Caligula, and Nero, Domitian, Commodus, Caracalla and Heliogabalus would never have been. It was he who gave them both raison d'etre and incentive. The lives of all of them are horrible, yet analyze the horrible and you find the sublime.

Fancy a peak piercing the heavens, shadowing the earth. It was on a peak such as that the young emperors of old Rome balanced themselves, a precipice on either side. Did they look below, a vertigo rose to meet them; from above delirium came, while the horizon, though it hemmed the limits of vision, could not mark the frontiers of their dream. In addition there was the exaltation that altitudes produce. The valleys have their imbeciles; it is from mountains the poet and madman come. Caligula was both, sceptred at that; and with what a sceptre! One that stretched from the Rhine to the Euphrates, dominated a hundred and fifty million people; one that a mattress had given and a knife was to take away; a sceptre that lashed the earth, threatened the sky, beckoned planets and ravished the divinity of the divine.

To wield such a sceptre securely requires grace, no doubt, majesty too, but certainly strength; the latter Caligula possessed, but it was the feverish strength of one who had fathomed the unfathomable, and who sought to make its depths his own. Caligula was haunted by the intangible. His sleep was a communion with Nature, with whom he believed himself one. At times the Ocean talked to him; at others the Earth had secrets which it wished to tell. Again there was some matter of moment which he must mention to the day, and he would wander out in the vast galleries of the palace and invoke the Dawn, bidding it come and listen to his speech. The day was deaf, but there was the moon, and he prayed her to descend and share his couch. Luna declined to be the mistress of a mortal; to seduce her Caligula determined to become a god.

Nothing was easier. An emperor had but to open his veins, and in an hour he was a divinity. But the divinity which Caligula desired was not of that kind. He wished to be a god, not on Olympus alone, but on earth as well. He wished to be a palpable, tangible, living god; one that mortals could see, which was more, he knew, than could be said of the others. The mere wish was sufficient--Rome fell at his feet. The patent of divinity was in the genuflections of a nation. At once he had a temple, priests and flamens. Inexhaustible Greece was sacked again. The statues of her gods, disembarked at Rome, were decapitated, and on them the head of Caius shone.

Heretofore his dress had not been Roman, nor, for that matter, the dress of a man. On his wrists were bracelets; about his shoulders was a mantle sewn with gems; beneath was a tunic, and on his feet were the high white slippers that women wore. But when the god came the costume changed. One day he was Apollo, the nimbus on his curls, the Graces at his side; the next he was Mercury, wings at his heels, the caduceus in his hand; again he was Venus. But it was as Jupiter Latialis, armed with the thunderbolt and decorated with a great gold beard, that he appeared at his best.

The role was very real to him. After the fashion of Olympians he became frankly incestuous, seducing vestals, his sisters too, and gaining in boldness with each metamorphosis, he menaced the Capitoline Jove. "Prove your power," he cried to him, "or fear my own!" He thundered at him with machine-made thunder, with lightning that flashed from a pan. "Kill me," he shouted, "or I will kill you!" Jove, unmoved, must have moved his assailant, for presently Caligula lowered his voice, whispered in the old god's ear, questioned him, meditated on his answer, grew perplexed, violent again, and threatened to send him home.

These interviews humanized him. He forgot the moon and mingled with men, inviting them to die. The invitation being invariably accepted, he became a connoisseur in death, an artist in blood, a ruler to whom cruelty was not merely an aid to government but an individual pleasure, and therewith such a perfect lover, such a charming host!

"Dear heart," he murmured to his mistress Pryallis, as she lay one night in his arms, "I think I will have you tortured that you may tell me why I love you so." But of that the girl saw no need. She either knew the reason or invented one, for presently he added: "And to think that I have but a sign to make and that beautiful head of yours is off!" Musings of this description were so humorous that one evening he explained to guests whom he had startled with his laughter, that it was amusing to reflect how easily he could have all of them killed.

But even to a god life is not an unmixed delight. Caligula had his troubles. About him there had settled a disturbing quiet. Rome was hushed, the world was very still. There was not so much as an earthquake. The reign of Augustus had been marked by the defeat of Varus. Under Tiberius a falling amphitheatre had killed a multitude. Caligula felt that through sheer felicity his own reign might be forgot. A famine, a pest, an absolute defeat, a terrific conflagration--any prodigious calamity that should sweep millions away and stamp his own memory immutably on the chronicles of time, how desirable it were! But there was nothing. The crops had never been more abundant; apart from the arenas and the prisons, the health of the empire was excellent; on the frontiers not so much as the rumor of an insurrection could be heard, and Nero was yet to come.

Perplexed, Caligula reflected, and presently from Baiae to Puzzoli, over the waters of the bay, he galloped on horseback, the cuirass of Alexander glittering on his breast. The intervening miles had been spanned by a bridge of ships and on them a road had been built, one of those roads for which the Romans were famous, a road like the Appian Way, in earth and stone, bordered by inns, by pink arcades, green retreats, forest reaches, the murmur of trickling streams. So many ships were anchored there that through the unrepleted granaries the fear of famine stalked. Caligula, meanwhile, his guests behind him, made cavalry charges across the sea, or in a circus-chariot held the ribbons, while four white horses, maddened by swaying lights, bore him to the other shore. At night the entire coast was illuminated; the bridge was one great festival, brilliant but brief. Caligula had wearied of it all. At a signal the multitude of guests he had assembled there were tossed into the sea.

By way of a souvenir, Tiberius, whom he murdered, had left him the immensity of his treasure. "I must be economical or Caesar," Caligula reflected, and tipped a coachman a million, rained on the people a hail of coin, bathed in essences, set before his guests loaves of silver, gold omelettes, sausages of gems; sailed to the hum of harps on a ship that had porticoes, gardens, baths, bowers, spangled sails and a jewelled prow; removed a mountain, and put a palace where it had been; filled in a valley and erected a temple on the top; supplied a horse with a marble home, with ivory stalls, with furniture and slaves; contemplated making him consul; made him a host instead, one that in his own equine name invited the fashion of Rome to sup with Incitatus.

In one year Tiberius' legacy, a sum that amounted to four hundred million of our money, was spent. Caligula had achieved the impossible; he was a bankrupt god, an emperor without a copper. But the very splendor of that triumph demanded a climax. If Caligula hesitated, no one knew it. On the morrow the palace of the Caesars was turned into a lupanar, a little larger, a little handsomer than the others, but still a brothel, one of which the inmates were matrons of Rome and the keeper Jupiter Latialis.

After that, seemingly, there was nothing save apotheosis. But Caligula, in the nick of time, remembered the ocean. At the head of an army he crossed Gaul, attacked it, and returned refreshed. Decidedly he had not exhausted everything yet. He recalled Tiberius' policy, and abruptly the world was filled again with accusers and accused. Gold poured in on him, the earth paid him tribute. In a vast hall he danced naked on the wealth of nations. Once more he was rich, richer than ever; there were still illusions to be looted, other dreams to be pierced; yet, even as he mused, conspirators were abroad. He loosed his pretorians. "Had Rome but one head!" he muttered. "Let them FEEL themselves die," he cried to his officers. "Let me be hated, but let me be feared."

One day, as he was returning from the theatre, the dagger did its usual work. Rome had lost a genius; in his place there came an ass.

There is a verse in Greek to the effect that the blessed have children in three months. Livia and Augustus were blessed in this pleasant fashion. Three months after their marriage a child was born--a miracle which surprised no one aware of their previous intimacy. The child became a man, and the father of Claud, an imbecile whom the pretorians, after Caligula's death, found in a closet, shaking with fright, and whom for their own protection they made emperor in his stead.

Caligula had been frankly adored; there was in him an originality, and with it a grandeur and a mad magnificence that enthralled. Then, too, he was young, and at his hours what the French call charmeur. If at times he frightened, always he dazzled. Of course he was adored; the prodigal emperors always were; so were their successors, the wicked popes. Man was still too near to nature to be aware of shame, and infantile enough to care to be surprised. In that was Caligula's charm; he petted his people and surprised them too. Claud wearied. Between them they assimilate every contradiction, and in their incoherences explain that incomprehensible chaos which was Rome. Caligula jeered at everybody; everybody jeered at Claud.

The latter was a fantastic, vacillating, abstracted, cowardly tyrant, issuing edicts in regard to the proper tarring of barrels, and rendering absurd decrees; declaring himself to be of the opinion of those who were right; falling asleep on the bench, and on awakening announcing that he gave judgment in favor of those whose reasons were the best; slapped in the face by an irritable plaintiff; held down by main force when he wanted to leave; inviting to supper those whom he had killed before breakfast; answering the mournful salute of the gladiators with a grotesque Avete vos--"Be it well too with you," a response, parenthetically, which the gladiators construed as a pardon and refused to fight; dowering the alphabet with three new letters which lasted no longer than he did; asserting that he would give centennial games as often as he saw fit; an emperor whom no one obeyed, whose eunuchs ruled in his stead, whose lackeys dispensed exiles, death, consulates and crucifixions; whose valets insulted the senate, insulted Rome, insulted the sovereign that ruled the world, whose people shared his consort's couch; a slipshod drunkard in a tattered gown--such was the imbecile that succeeded Caligula and had Messalina for wife.

It were curious to have seen that woman as Juvenal did, a veil over her yellow wig, hunting adventures through the streets of Rome, while her husband in the Forum censured the dissoluteness of citizens. And it were curious, too, to understand whether it was her audacity or his stupidity which left him the only man in Rome unacquainted with the prodigious multiplicity and variety of her lovers. History has its secrets, yet, in connection with Messalina, there is one that historians have not taken the trouble to probe; to them she has been an imperial strumpet. Messalina was not that. At heart she was probably no better and no worse than any other lady of the land, but pathologically she was an unbalanced person, who to-day would be put through a course of treatment, instead of being put to death. When Claud at last learned, not the truth, but that some of her lovers were conspiring to get rid of him, he was not indignant; he was frightened. The conspirators were promptly disposed of, Messalina with them. Suetonius says that, a few days later, as he went in to supper, he asked why the empress did not appear.

Apart from the neurosis from which she suffered, were it possible to find an excuse for her conduct, the excuse would be Claud. The purple which made Caligula mad, made him an idiot; and when in course of time he was served with a succulent poison, there must have been many conjectures in Rome as to what the empire would next produce.

The empire was extremely fecund, enormously vast. About Rome extended an immense circle of provinces and cities that were wholly hers. Without that circle was another, the sovereignty exercised over vassals and allies; beyond that, beyond the Rhine on one side, were the silenced Teutons; beyond the Euphrates on the other, the hazardous Parthians, while remotely to the north there extended the enigmas of barbarism; to the south, those semi-fabulous regions where geography ceased to be.

Little by little, through the patience of a people that felt itself eternal, this immensity had been assimilated and fused. A few fortresses and legions on the frontiers, a stretch of soldiery at any spot an invasion might be feared; a little tact, a maternal solicitude, and that was all. Rome governed unarmed, or perhaps it might be more exact to say she did not govern at all; she was the mistress of a federation of realms and republics that governed themselves, in whose government she was content, and from whom she exacted little, tribute merely, and obeisance to herself. Her strength was not in the sword; the lioness roared rarely, often slept; it was the fear smaller beasts had of her awakening that made them docile; once aroused those indolent paws could do terrible work, and it was well not to excite them. When the Jews threatened to revolt, Agrippa warned them: "Look at Rome; look at her well; her arms are invisible, her troops are afar; she rules, not by them, but by the certainty of her power. If you rebel, the invisible sword will flash, and what can you do against Rome armed, when Rome unarmed frightens the world?"

The argument was pertinent and suggestive, but the secret of Rome's ascendency consisted in the fact that where she conquered she dwelt. Wherever the eagles pounced, Rome multiplied herself in miniature. In the army was the nation, in the legion the city. Where it camped, presto! a judgment seat and an altar. On the morrow there was a forum; in a week there were paved avenues; in a fortnight, temples, porticoes; in a month you felt yourself at home. Rome built with a magic that startled as surely as the glint of her sword. Time and again the nations whom Caesar encountered planned to eliminate his camp. When they reached it the camp had vanished; in its place was a walled, impregnable town.

As the standards lowered before that town, the pomoerium was traced. Within it the veteran found a home, without it a wife; and the family established, the legion that had conquered the soil with the sword, subsisted on it with the plow. Presently there were priests there, aqueducts, baths, theatres and games, all the marvel of imperial elegance and vice. When the aborigine wandered that way, his seduction was swift.

The enemy that submitted became a subject, not a slave. Rome commanded only the free. If his goods were taxed, his goods remained his own, his personal liberty untrammelled. His land had become part of a new province, it is true, but provided he did not interest himself in such matters as peace and war, not only was he free to manage his own affairs, but that land, were it at the uttermost end of the earth, might, in recompense of his fidelity, come to be regarded as within the Italian territory; as such, sacred, inviolate, free from taxes, and he a citizen of Rome, senator even, emperor!

Conquest once solidified, the rest was easy. Tattered furs were replaced by the tunic and uncouth idioms by the niceties of Latin speech. In some cases, where the speech had been beaten in with the hilt of the sword, the accent was apt to be rough, but a generation, two at most, and there were sweethearts and swains quoting Horace in the moonlight, naively unaware that only the verse of the Greeks could pleasure the Roman ear.

The principalities and kingdoms that of their own wish [a wish often suggested, and not always amicably either] became allies of Rome and mingled their freedom with hers, entered into an alliance whereby in return for Rome's patronage and protection they agreed to have a proper regard for the dignity of the Roman people and to have no other friends or enemies than those that were Rome's--a formula exquisite in the civility with which it exacted the renunciation of every inherent right. A king wrote to the senate: "I have obeyed your deputy as I would have obeyed a god." "And you have done wisely," the senate answered, a reply which, in its terseness, tells all.

Diplomacy and the plow, such were Rome's methods. As for herself she fought, she did not till. Italy, devastated by the civil wars, was uncultivated, cut up into vast unproductive estates. From one end to the other there was barely a trace of agriculture, not a sign of traffic. You met soldiers, cooks, petty tradesmen, gladiators, philosophers, patricians, market gardeners, lazzaroni and millionaires; the merchant and the farmer, never. Rome's resources were in distant commercial centres, in taxes and tribute; her wealth had come of pillage and exaction. Save her strength, she had nothing of her own. Her religion, literature, art, philosophy, luxury and corruption, everything had come from abroad. In Greece were her artists; in Africa, Gaul and Spain, her agriculturists; in Asia her artisans. Her own breasts were sterile. When she gave birth it was to a litter of monsters, sometimes to a genius, by accident to a poet. She consumed, she did not produce. It was because of that she fell.

V
NERO

"Save a monster, what can you expect from Agrippina and myself?"

It was Domitius, Nero's father, who made this ingenious remark. He was not a good man; he was not even good-looking, merely vicious and rich. But his viciousness was benign beside that of Agrippina, who poisoned him when Nero's birth ensured the heritage of his wealth.

In all its galleries history has no other portrait such as hers. Caligula's sister, his mistress as well, exiled by him and threatened with death, her eyes dazzled and her nerves unstrung by the impossibilities of that fabulous reign, it was not until Claud, her uncle, recalled her and Messalina disappeared, that the empress awoke. She too, she determined, would rule, and the jus osculi aiding, she married out of hand that imbecile uncle of hers, on whose knee she had played as a child.

The day of the wedding a young patrician, expelled from the senate, killed himself. Agrippina had accused him of something not nice, not because he was guilty, nor yet because the possibility of the thing shocked her, but because he was betrothed to Octavia, Claud's daughter, who, Agrippina determined, should be Nero's wife. Presently Caligula's widow, an old rival of her own, a lady who had thought she would like to be empress twice, and whom Claud had eyed grotesquely, was disencumbered of three million worth of emeralds, with which she heightened her beauty, and told very civilly that it was time to die. So, too, disappeared a Calpurina, a Lepida; women young, rich, handsome, impure, and as such dangerous to Agrippina's peace of mind. The legality of her crimes was so absolute that the mere ownership of an enviable object was a cause for death. A senator had a villa which pleased her; he was invited to die. Another had a pair of those odorous murrhine vases, which Pompey had found in Armenia, and which on their first appearance set Rome wild; he, too, was invited to die.

But, though Agrippina dealt in death, she dealt in seductions too. Rome, that had adored Caligula, promptly fell under his sister's sway. There was a splendor in her eyes, which so many crimes had lit; in her carriage there was such majesty, the pomp with which she surrounded herself was so magnificent, that Rome, enthralled, applauded. Beyond, on the Rhine, a city which is today Cologne, rose in honor of her sovereignty. To her wishes the senate was subservient, to her indiscretions blind. Claud, who meanwhile had been wholly sightless, suddenly showed signs of discernment. A woman, charged with illicit commerce, was brought to his tribunal. He condemned her, of course. "In my case," he explained, "matrimony has not been successful, but the fate that destined me to marry impure women destined me also to punish them." It was then that Agrippina ordered of Locusta that famous stew of poison and mushrooms, which Nero, in allusion to Claud's apotheosis, called the food of the gods. The fate that destined Claud to marry Agrippina destined her to kill him.

It was under her care, between a barber and a ballerine, amid the shamelessness of his stepfather's palace, where any day he could have seen his mother beckon indolently to a centurion and pointing to some lover who had ceased to please, make the gesture which signified Death, that the young Enobarbus--Nero, as he subsequently called himself--was trained for the throne.

He had entered the world like a tiger cub, feet first; a circumstance which is said to have disturbed his mother, and well it might. During his adolescence that lady made herself feared. He was but seventeen when the pretorians called upon him to rule the world; and at the time an ingenuous lad, one who blushed like Lalage, very readily, particularly at the title of Father of the Country, which the senate was anxious to give him; endowed with excellent instincts, which he had got no one knew whence; a trifle petit maitre, perhaps, perfuming the soles of his feet, and careful about the arrangement of his yellow curls, but withal generous, modest, sympathetic--in short, a flower in a cesspool, a youth not over well-fitted to reign. But his mother was there; as he developed so did his fear of her, to such proportions even that he gave certain orders, and his mother was killed. That duel between mother and son, terrible in its intensity and unnameable horror, even the Borgias could not surpass. Tacitus has told it, dramatically, as was his wont, but he told it in Latin, in which tongue it had best remain.

At that time the ingenuous lad had disappeared. The cub was full-grown. Besides, he had tasted blood. Octavia, who with her brother, Britannicus, and her sister, Antonia, had been his playmates; who was almost his own sister; whose earliest memories interlinked with his, and who had become his wife, had been put to death; not that she had failed to please, but because a lady, Sabina Poppoea, who, Tacitus says, lacked nothing except virtue, had declined to be his mistress. At the time Sabina was married. But divorce was easy. Sabina got one at the bar; Nero with the axe. The twain were then united. Nero seems to have loved her greatly, a fact, as Suetonius puts it, which did not prevent him from kicking her to death. Already he had poisoned Britannicus, and with Octavia decapitated and Agrippina gone, of the imperial house there remained but Antonia and himself. The latter he invited to marry him; she declined. He invited her to die. He was then alone, the last of his race. Monsters never engender. A thinker who passed that way thought him right to have killed his mother; her crime was in giving him birth.

Therewith he was popular; more so even than Caligula, who was a poet, and as such apart from the crowd, while Nero was frankly canaille--well-meaning at that--which Caligula never was. During the early years of his reign he could not do good enough. The gladiators were not permitted to die; he would have no shedding of blood; the smell of it was distasteful. He would listen to no denunciations; when a decree of death was brought to him to sign, he regretted that he knew how to write. Rome had never seen a gentler prince, nor yet one more splendidly lavish. The people had not only the necessities of life, but the luxuries, the superfluities, too. For days and days in the Forum there was an incessant shower of tickets that were exchangeable, not for bread or trivial sums, but for gems, pictures, slaves, fortunes, ships, villas and estates. The creator of that shower was bound to be adored.

It was that, no doubt, which awoke him. A city like Rome, one that had over a million inhabitants, could make a terrific noise, and when that noise was applause, the recipient found it heady. Nero got drunk on popularity, and heredity aiding where the prince had been emerged the cad, a poseur that bored, a beast that disgusted, a caricature of the impossible in a crimson frame.

"What an artist the world is to lose!" he exclaimed as he died; and artist he was, but in the Roman sense; one that enveloped in the same contempt the musician, acrobat and actor. It was the artist that played the flute while gladiators died and lovers embraced; it was the artist that entertained the vulgar.

As an artist Nero might have been a card. Fancy the attraction--an emperor before the footlights; but fancy the boredom also. The joy at the announcement of his first appearance was so great that thanks were offered to the gods; and the verses he was to sing, graven in gold, were dedicated to the Capitoline Jove. The joy was brief. The exits of the theatre were closed. It was treason to attempt to leave. People pretended to be dead in order to be carried out, and well they might. The star was a fat man with a husky tenorino voice, who sang drunk and half-naked to a protecting claque of ten thousand hands.

But it was in the circus that Nero was at his best; there, no matter though he were last in the race, it was to him the palm was awarded, or rather it was he that awarded the palm to himself, and then quite magnificently shouted, "Nero, Caesar, victor in the race, gives his crown to the People of Rome!"

On the stage he had no rivals, and by chance did one appear, he was invited to die. In that respect he was artistically susceptible. When he turned acrobat, the statues of former victors were tossed in the latrinae. Yet, as competitors were needed, and moreover as he, singly, could fill neither a stage nor a track, it was the nobility of Rome that he ordered to appear with him. For that the nobility never forgave him. On the other hand, the proletariat loved him the better. What greater salve could it have than the sight of the conquerors of the world entertaining the conquered, lords amusing their lackeys?

Greece meanwhile sent him crowns and prayers; crowns for anticipated victories, prayers that he would come and win them. Homage so delicate was not to be disdained. Nero set forth, an army at his heels; a legion of claquers, a phalanx of musicians, cohorts of comedians, and with these for retinue, through sacred groves that Homer knew, through intervales which Hesiod sang, through a year of festivals he wandered, always victorious. It was he who conquered at Olympia; it was he who conquered at Corinth. No one could withstand him. Alone in history he won in every game, and with eighteen hundred crowns as trophies of war he repeated Caesar's triumph. In a robe immaterial as a moonbeam, the Olympian wreath on his curls, the Isthmian laurel in his hand, his army behind him, the clown that was emperor entered Rome. Victims were immolated as he passed, the Via Sacra was strewn with saffron, the day was rent with acclaiming shouts. Throughout the empire sacrifices were ordered. Old people that lived in the country fancied him, Philostratus says, the conqueror of new nations, and sacrificed with delight.

But if as artist he bored everybody, he was yet an admirable impresario. The spectacles he gave were unique. At one which was held in the Taurian amphitheatre it must have been delightful to assist. Fancy eighty thousand people on ascending galleries, protected from the sun by a canopy of spangled silk; an arena three acres large carpeted with sand, cinnabar and borax, and in that arena death in every form, on those galleries colossal delight.

The lowest gallery, immediately above the arena, was a wide terrace where the senate sat. There were the dignitaries of the empire, and with them priests in their sacerdotal robes; vestals in linen, their hair arranged in the six braids that were symbolic of virginity; swarms of Oriental princes, rainbows of foreign ambassadors; and in the centre, the imperial pulvinar, an enclosed pavilion, in which Nero lounged, a mignon at his feet.

In the gallery above were the necklaced knights, their tunics bordered with the augusticlave, their deep-blue cloaks fastened to the shoulder; and there, too, in their wide white togas, were the citizens of Rome.

Still higher the people sat. In the topmost gallery were the women, and in a separate enclosure a thousand musicians answered the cries of the multitude with the blare and the laugh of brass.

Beneath the terraces, behind the barred doors that punctuated the marble wall which circled the arena, were Mauritian panthers that had been entrapped with rotten meat; hippopotami from Sais, lured by the smell of carrots into pits; the rhinoceros of Gaul, taken with the net; lions, lassoed in the deserts; Lucanian bears, Spanish bulls; and, in remoter dens, men, unarmed, that waited.

By way of foretaste for better things, a handful of criminals, local desperadoes, an impertinent slave, a machinist, who in a theatre the night before had missed an effect--these, together with a negligent usher, were tossed one after the other naked into the ring, and bound to a scaffold that surmounted a miniature hill. At a signal the scaffold fell, the hill crumbled, and from it a few hyenas issued, who indolently devoured their prey.

With this for prelude, the gods avenged and justice appeased, a rhinoceros ambled that way, stimulated from behind by the point of a spear; and in a moment the hyenas were disembowelled, their legs quivering in the air. Throughout the arena other beasts, tied together with long cords, quarrelled in couples; there was the bellow of bulls, and the moan of leopards tearing at their flesh, a flight of stags, and the long, clean spring of the panther.

Presently the arena was cleared, the sand reraked and the Bestiarii advanced--Sarmatians, nourished on mares' milk; Sicambrians, their hair done up in chignons; horsemen from Thessaly, Ethiopian warriors, Parthian archers, huntsmen from the steppes, their different idioms uniting in a single cry--"Caesar, we salute you." The sunlight, filtering through the spangled canopy, chequered their tunics with burning spots, danced on their spears and helmets, dazzled the spectators' eyes. From above descended the caresses of flutes; the air was sweet with perfumes, alive with multi-colored motes; the terraces were parterres of blending hues, and into that splendor a hundred lions, their tasselled tails sweeping the sand, entered obliquely.

The mob of the Bestiarii had gone. In the middle of the arena, a band of Ethiopians, armed with arrows, knives and spears, knelt, their oiled black breasts uncovered.

Leisurely the lions turned their huge, intrepid heads; to their jowls wide creases came. There was a glitter of fangs, a shiver that moved the mane, a flight of arrows, mounting murmurs; the crouch of beasts preparing to spring, a deafening roar, and, abruptly, a tumultuous mass, the suddenness of knives, the snap of bones, the cry of the agonized, the fury of beasts transfixed, the shrieks of the mangled, a combat hand to fang, from which lions fell back, their jaws torn asunder, while others retreated, a black body swaying between their terrible teeth, and, insensibly, a descending quiet.

At once there was an eruption of bellowing elephants, painted and trained for slaughter, that trampled on wounded and dead. At a call from a keeper the elephants disappeared. There was a rush of mules and slaves; the carcasses and corpses vanished, the toilet of the ring was made; then came a plunge of bulls, mists of vapor about their long, straight horns, their anxious eyes dilated. Beyond was a troop of Thessalians. For a moment the bulls snorted, pawing the sand with their fore-feet, as though trying to realize what they were doing there. Yet instantly they seemed to know, and with lowered heads, they plunged on the point of spears. But no matter, horses went down by the hundred; and as the bulls tired of gorging the dead, they fought each other; fought rancorously, fought until weariness overtook them, and the surviving Thessalians leaped on their backs, twisted their horns, and threw them down, a sword through their throbbing throats.

Successively the arena was occupied by bears, by panthers, by dogs trained for the chase, by hunters and hunted. But the episode of the morning was a dash of wild elephants, attacked on either side; a moment of sheer delight, in which the hunters were tossed up on the terraces, tossed back again by the spectators, and trampled to death.

With that for bouquet the first part of the performance was at an end. By way of interlude, the ring was peopled with acrobats, who flew up in the air like birds, formed pyramids together, on the top of which little boys swung and smiled. There was a troop of trained lions, their manes gilded, that walked on tight-ropes, wrote obscenities in Greek, and danced to cymbals which one of them played. There were geese-fights, wonderful combats between dwarfs and women; a chariot race, in which bulls, painted white, held the reins, standing upright while drawn at full speed; a chase of ostriches, and feats of haute ecole on zebras from Madagascar.

The interlude at an end, the sand was reraked, and preceded by the pomp of lictors, interminable files of gladiators entered, holding their knives to Nero that he might see that they were sharp. It was then the eyes of the vestals lighted; artistic death was their chiefest joy, and in a moment, when the spectacle began and the first gladiator fell, above the din you could hear their cry "Hic habet!" and watch their delicate thumbs reverse.

There was no cowardice in that arena. If by chance any hesitation were discernible, instantly there were hot irons, the sear of which revivified courage at once. But that was rare. The gladiators fought for applause, for liberty, for death; fought manfully, skilfully, terribly, too, and received the point of the sword or the palm of the victor, their expression unchanged, the face unmoved. Among them, some provided with a net and prodigiously agile, pursued their adversaries hither and thither, trying to entangle them first and kill them later. Others, protected by oblong shields and armed with short, sharp swords, fought hand-to-hand. There were still others, mailed horsemen, who fought with the lance, and charioteers that dealt death from high Briton cars.

As a spectacle it was unique; one that the Romans, or more exactly, their predecessors, the Etruscans, had devised to train their children for war and allay the fear of blood. It had been serviceable, indeed, and though the need of it had gone, still the institution endured, and in enduring constituted the chief delight of the vestals and of Rome. By means of it a bankrupt became consul and an emperor beloved. It had stayed revolutions, it was the tax of the proletariat on the rich. Silver and bread were for the individual, but these things were for the crowd.

During the pauses of the combats the dead were removed by men masked as Mercury, god of hell; red irons, that others, masked as Charon, bore, being first applied as safeguard against swoon or fraud. And when, to the kisses of flutes, the last palm had been awarded, the last death acclaimed, a ballet was given; that of Paris and Venus, which Apuleius has described so well, and for afterpiece the romance of Pasipha? and the bull. Then, as night descended, so did torches, too; the arena was strewn with vermilion; tables were set, and to the incitement of crotals, Lydians danced before the multitude, toasting the last act of that wonderful day.

It was with such magnificence that Nero showed the impresario's skill, the politician's adroitness. Where the artist, which he claimed to be, really appeared, was in the refurbishing of Rome.

In spite of Augustus' boast, the city was not by any means of marble. It was filled with crooked little streets, with the atrocities of the Tarquins, with houses unsightly and perilous, with the moss and dust of ages; it compared with Alexandria as London compares with Paris; it had a splendor of its own, but a splendor that could be heightened.

Whether the conflagration which occurred at that time was the result of accident or design is uncertain and in any event immaterial. Tacitus says that when it began Nero was at Antium, in which case he must have hastened to return, for admitting that he did not originate the fire, it is a matter of agreement that he collaborated in it. In quarters where it showed symptoms of weakness it was by his orders coaxed to new strength; colossal stone buildings, on which it had little effect, were battered down with catapults.

Fire is a perfect poet. No designer ever imagined the surprises it creates, and when, at the end of the week, three-fourths of the city was in ruins, the beauty that reigned there must have been sublime. That it inspired Nero is presumable. The palace on the Palatine, which Tiberius embellished and Caligula enlarged, had gone; in its place rose another, aflame with gold. Before it Neropolis extended, a city of triumphal arches, enchanted temples, royal dwellings, shimmering porticoes, glittering roofs, and wide, hospitable streets. It was fair to the eye, purely

Greek; and on its heart, from the Circus Maximus to the Forum's edge, the new and gigantic palace shone. Before it was a lake, a part of which Vespasian drained and replaced with an amphitheatre that covered eight acres. About that lake were separate edifices that formed a city in themselves; between them and the palace, a statue of Nero in gold and silver mounted precipitately a hundred and twenty feet--a statue which it took twenty-four elephants to move. About it were green savannahs, forest reaches, the call of bird and deer, while in the distance, fronted by a stretch of columns a mile in length, the palace stood--a palace so ineffably charming that on the day of reckoning may it outbalance a few of his sins. Even the cellars were frescoed. The baths were quite comfortable; you had waters salt or sulphurous at will. The dining halls had ivory ceilings from which flowers fell, and wainscots that changed at each service. The walls were alive with the glisten of gems, with marbles rarer than jewels. In one hall was a dome of sapphire, a floor of malachite, crystal columns and red-gold walls.

"At last," Nero murmured, "I am lodged like a man."

No doubt. Yet in a mirror he would have seen a bloated beast in a flowered gown, the hair done up in a chignon, the skin covered with eruptions, the eyes circled and yellow; a woman who had hours when she imitated a virgin at bay, others when she was wife, still others when she expected to be a mother, and that woman, a senatorial patent of divinity aiding, was god--Apollo's peer, imperator, chief of the army, pontifix maximus, master of the world, with the incontestable right of life and death over every being in the dominions.

It had taken the fresh-faced lad who blushed so readily, just fourteen years to effect that change. Did he regret it? And what should Nero regret? Nothing, perhaps, save that at the moment when he declared himself to be lodged like a man, he had not killed himself like one. But of that he was incapable. Had he known what the future held, possibly he might have imitated that apotheosis of vulgarity in which Sardanapalus eclipsed himself, but never could he have died with the good breeding and philosophy of Cato, for neither good breeding nor philosophy was in him. Nero killed himself like a coward, yet that he did kill himself, in no matter what fashion, is one of the few things that can be said in his favor.

Those days differed from ours. There were circumstances in which suicide was regarded as the simplest of duties. Nero did his duty, but not until he was forced to it, and even then not until he had been asked several times whether it was so hard to die. The empire had wearied of him. In Neropolis his popularity had gone as popularity ever does; the conflagration had killed it.

Even as he wandered, lyre in hand, a train of Lesbians and pederasts at his heels, through those halls which had risen on the ruins, and which inexhaustible Greece had furnished with a fresh crop of white immortals, the world rebelled. Afar on the outskirts of civilization a vassal, ashamed of his vassalage, declared war, not against Rome, but against an emperor that played the flute. In Spain, in Gaul, the legions were choosing other chiefs. The provinces, depleted by imperial exactions, outwearied by the increasing number of accusers, whose accusations impoverishing them served only to multiply the prodigalities of their Caesar, revolted.

Suddenly Nero found himself alone. As the advancing rumor of rebellion reached him, he thought of flight; there was no one that would accompany him. He called to the pretorians; they would not hear. Through the immensity of his palace he sought one friend. The doors would not open. He returned to his apartment; the guards had gone. Then terror seized him. He was afraid to die, afraid to live, afraid of his solitude, afraid of Rome, afraid of himself; but what frightened him most was that everyone had lost their fear of him. It was time to go, and a slave aiding, he escaped in disguise from Rome, and killed himself, reluctantly, in a hovel.

"Qualis artifex pereo!" he is reported to have muttered. Say rather, qualis maechus.

VI
THE HOUSE OF FLAVIA

It was in those days that the nebulous figure of Apollonius of Tyana appeared and disappeared in Rome. His speech, a commingling of puerility and charm, Philostratus has preserved. Rumor had preceded him. It was said that he knew everything, save the caresses of women; that he was familiar with all languages; with the speech of bird and beast; with that of silence, for silence is a language too; that he had prayed in the Temple of Jupiter Lycoeus, where men lost their shadows, their lives as well; that he had undergone eighty initiations of Mithra; that he had perplexed the magi; confuted the gymnosophists; that he foretold the future, healed the sick, raised the dead; that beyond the Himalayas he had encountered every species of ferocious beast, except the tyrant, and that it was to see one that he had come to Rome.

Nero was quite free from prejudice. Apart from a doll which he worshipped he had no superstitions. He had the plain man's dislike of philosophy; Seneca had sickened him of it, perhaps; but he was sensitive, not that he troubled himself particularly about any lies that were told of him, but he did object to people who went about telling the truth. In that respect he was not unique; we are all like him, but he had ways of stilling the truth which were imperial and his own.

Promptly on Apollonius he loosed his bull-dog, Tigellin, prefect of police.

Tigellin caught him. "What have you with you?" he asked.

"Continence, Justice, Temperance, Strength and Patience," Apollonius answered.

"Your slaves, I suppose. Make out a list of them."

Apollonius shook his head. "They are not my slaves; they are my masters."

"There is but one," Tigellin retorted--"Nero. Why do you not fear him?"

"Because the god that made him terrible made me without fear."

"I will leave you your liberty," muttered the startled Tigellin, "but you must give bail."

"And who," asked Apollonius superbly, "would bail a man whom no one can enchain?" Therewith he turned and disappeared.

At that time Nero was in training to suffocate a lion in the arena. A few days later he killed himself. Simultaneously there came news from Syracuse. A woman of rank had given birth to a child with three heads. Apollonius examined it.

"There will be three emperors at once," he announced. "But their reign will be shorter than that of kings on the stage."

Within that year Galba, who was emperor for an instant, died at the gates of Rome. Vitellius, after being emperor in little else than dream, was butchered in the Forum; and Otho, in that fine antique fashion, killed himself in Gaul. Apollonius meanwhile was in Alexandria, predicting the purple to Vespasian, the rise of the House of Flavia; invoking Jupiter in his protege's behalf; and presently, the prediction accomplished, he was back in Rome, threatening Domitian, warning him that the House of Flavia would fall.

The atmosphere was then charged with the marvellous; the world was filled with prodigies, with strange gods, beckoning chimeras and credulous crowds. Belief in the supernatural was absolute; the occult sciences, astrology, magic, divination, all had their adepts. In Greece there were oracles at every turn, and with them prophets who taught the art of adultery and how to construe the past. On the banks of the Rhine there were girls who were regarded as divinities, and in Gaul were men who were held wholly divine.

Jerusalem too had her follies. There was Simon the Magician, founder of gnosticism, father of every heresy, Messiah to the Jews, Jupiter to the Gentiles--an impudent self-made god, who pretended to float in the air, and called his mistress Minerva--a deification, parenthetically, which was accepted by Nicholas, his successor, a deacon of the church, who raised her to the eighth heaven as patron saint of lust. To him, as to Simon, she was Ennoia, Prunikos, Helen of Troy. She had been Delilah, Lucretia. She had prostituted herself to every nation; she had sung in the by-ways, and hidden robbers in the vermin of her bed. But by Simon she was rehabilitated. It was she, no doubt, of whom Caligula thought when he beckoned to the moon. In Rome she had her statue, and near it was one to Simon, the holy god.

But of all manifestations of divinity the most patent was that which haloed Vespasian. He expected it, Suetonius says, but it is doubtful if any one else did. One night he dreamed that an era of prosperity was to dawn for him and his when Nero lost a tooth. The next day he was shown one which had been drawn from the emperor's mouth. But that was nothing. Presently at Carmel the Syrian oracle assured him that he would be successful in whatever he undertook. From Rome word came that, while the armies of Vitellius and Otho were fighting, two eagles had fought above them, and that the victor had been despatched by a third eagle that had come from the East. In Alexandria Serapis whispered to him. The entire menagerie of Egypt proclaimed him king. Apis bellowed, Anubis barked. Isis visited him unveiled. The lame and the blind pressed about him; he cured them with a touch. There could be no reasonable doubt now; surely he was a god. On his shoulders Apollonius threw the purple, and Vespasian set out for Rome.

His antecedents were less propitious. The descendant of an obscure centurion, he had been a veterinary surgeon; then, having got Caligula's ear, he flattered it abominably. Caligula disposed of, he flattered Claud, or what amounted to the same thing, Narcissus, Claud's chamberlain. Through the influence of the latter he became a lieutenant, fought on remote frontiers--fought well, too--so well even that, Narcissus gone, he felt Agrippina watching him, and knowing the jealousy of her eyes, prudently kept quiet until that lady did.

With Nero he promenaded through Greece--sat at the Olympian games and fell asleep when his emperor sang. Treason of that high nature--sacrilege, rather, for Nero was then a god--might have been overlooked, had it occurred but once, for Nero could be magnanimous when he chose. But it always occurred. To Nero's tremolo invariably came the accompaniment of Vespasian's snore. He was dreaming of that tooth, no doubt. "I am not a soporific, am I?" Nero gnashed at him, and sent the blasphemer away.

For a while Vespasian lived in constant expectation of some civil message inviting him to die. Finally it came, only he was invited to die at the head of an army which Nero had projected against seditious Jews. When he returned, leaving his son Titus to attend to Jerusalem, it was as emperor.

Only a moment before Vitellius had been disposed of. That curious glutton, whom the Rhenish legions had chosen because of his coarse familiarity, would willingly have fled had the soldiery let him. But not at all; they wanted a prince of their own manufacture. They knew nothing of Vespasian, cared less; and into the Capitol they chased the latter's partisans, his son Domitian as well. The besieged defended themselves with masterpieces, with sacred urns, the statues of gods, the pedestals of divinities. Suddenly the Capitol was aflame. Simultaneously Vespasian's advance guard beat at the gates. The besiegers turned, the mob was with them, and together they fought, first at the gates, then in the streets, in the Forum, retreating always, but like lions, their face to the foe. The volatile mob, noting the retreat, turned from combatant into spectator. Let the soldiers fight; it was their duty, not theirs; and, as the struggle continued, from roof and window they eyed it with that artistic delight which the arena had developed, applauding the clever thrusts, abusing the vanquished, robbing the dead, and therewith pillaging the wineshops, crowding the lupanars. During the orgy, Vitellius was stabbed. The Flavians had won the day, the empire was Vespasian's.

The use he made of it was very modest. In spite of his manifest divinity he had nothing in common with the Caesars that had gone before; he had no dreams of the impossible, no desire to frighten Jupiter or seduce the moon. He was a plain man, tall and ruddy, very coarse in speech and thought, open-armed and close-fisted, slapping senators on the back and keeping a sharp eye on the coppers; taxing the latrinae, and declaring that money had no smell; yet still, in comparison with Claud and Nero, almost the ideal; absolutely uninteresting also, yet doing what good he could; effacing at once the traces of the civil war, rebuilding the Capitol; calming the people, protecting the provinces, restoring to Rome the gardens of Nero, clipping the wings of the Palace of Gold, throwing open again the Via Sacra, over which the Palace had spread; draining the lake that had shimmered before it, and erecting the Colosseum in its place.

In spite of Serapsis, Anubis and Isis, he had not the faintest odor of myth about him; absolutely bourgeois, he lacked even that atmosphere of burlesque that surrounded Claud; he was not even vicious. But he was a soldier, a brave one; and if, with the acquired economy of a subaltern who has been obliged to live on his pay, he kept his purse-strings tight, they were loose enough if a friend were in need, and he paid no one the compliment of a lie. He was projected sheer out of the republic. The better part of his life had been passed under arms; the delicate sensuality of Rome was foreign to him. It was there that Domitian had lived.

It were interesting to have watched that young man killing flies by the hour, while he meditated on the atrocities he was to commit--atrocities so numberless and needless that in the red halls of the Caesars he has left a portrait which is unique. Slender, graceful, handsome, as were all the young emperors of old Rome, his blue, troubled eyes took pleasure, if at all, only in the sight of blood.

In accordance with the fashion which Caligula and Nero had set, Domitian's earliest manners were those of an urbane and gentle prince. Later, when he made it his turn to rule, informers begged their bread in exile. Where they are not punished, he announced, they are encouraged. The sacrifices were so distressing to him that he forbade the immolation of oxen. He was disinterested, too, refusing legacies when the testator left nearer heirs, and therewith royally generous, covering his suite with presents, and declaring that to him avarice of all vices was the lowest and most vile. In short, you would have said another adolescent Nero come to Rome; there was the same silken sweetness of demeanor, the same ready blush, in addition to a zeal for justice and equity which other young emperors had been too thought-less to show.

His boyhood, too, had not been above reproach. The same things were whis-pered about him that had been shouted at Augustus. Manifestly he lacked not one of the qualities which go to the making of a model prince. Vespasian alone had his doubts.

"Mushrooms won't hurt you," he cried one day, as Domitian started at the sight of a ragout a la Sardanapale, which he fancied, possibly, was a la Locuste, "It is steel you should fear."

At that time, with a father for emperor and a brother who was sacking Jerusa-lem, Domitian had but one cause for anxiety, to wit--that the empire might escape him. It was then he began his meditations over holocausts of flies. For hours he secluded himself, occupied solely with their slaughter. He treated them precisely as Titus treated the Jews, enjoying the quiver of their legs, the little agonies of their silent death.

Tiberius had been in love with solitude, but never as he. Night after night he wandered on the terraces of the palace, watching the red moon wane white, com-panioned only by his dreams, those waking dreams that poets and madmen share, that Pallas had him in her charge, that Psyche was amorous of his eyes.

Meanwhile he was a nobody, a young gentleman merely, who might have moved in the best society, and who preferred the worst--his own. The sudden ele-vation of Vespasian preoccupied him, and while he knew that in the natural course of events his father would move to Olympus, yet there was his brother Titus, on whose broad shoulders the mantle of purple would fall. If the seditious Jews only knew their business! But no. Forty years before a white apparition on the way to Golgotha had cried to a handful of women, "The days are coming in which they shall say to the mountains, 'Fall on us'; to the hills, 'Cover us.'" And the days had come. A million of them had been butchered. From the country they had fled to the city; from Acra they had climbed to Zion. When the city burst into flames their blood put it out. Decidedly they did not know their business. Titus, instead of being stabbed before Jerusalem's walls, was marching in triumph to Rome.

The procession that presently entered the gates was a stream of splendor; crowns of rubies and gold; garments that glistened with gems; gods on their sacred pedestals; prisoners; curious beasts; Jerusalem in miniature; pictures of war; booty from the Temple, the veil, the candelabra, the cups of gold and the Book of the Law. To the rear rumbled the triumphal car, in which laurelled and mantled Titus stood, Vespasian at his side; while, in the distance, on horseback, came Domitian--a supernumerary, ignored by the crowd.

When the prisoners disappeared in the Tullianum and a herald shouted, "They have lived!" Domitian returned to the palace and hunted morosely for flies. The excesses of the festival in which Rome was swooning then had no delights for him. Presently the moon would rise, and then on the deserted terrace perhaps he would bathe a little in her light, and dream again of Pallas and of the possibilities of an emperor's sway, but meanwhile those blue troubled eyes that Psyche was amorous of were filled with envy and with hate. It was not that he begrudged Titus the triumph. The man who had disposed of a million Jews deserved not one triumph, but ten. It was the purple that haunted him.

Domitian was then in the early twenties. The Temple of Peace was ascending; the Temple of Janus was closed; the empire was at rest. Side by side with Vespasian, Titus ruled. From the Euphrates came the rumor of some vague revolt. Domitian thought he would like to quell it. He was requested to keep quiet. It occurred to him that his father ought to be ashamed of himself to reign so long. He was requested to vacate his apartment. There were dumb plots in dark cellars, of which only the echo of a whisper has descended to us, but which at the time were quite loud enough to reach Vespasian's ears. Titus interceded. Domitian was requested to behave.

For a while he prowled in the moonlight. He had been too precipitate, he decided, and to allay suspicion presently he went about in society, mingling his hours with those of married women. Manifestly his ways had mended. But Vespasian was uneasy. A comet had appeared. The doors of the imperial mausoleum had opened of themselves, besides, he was not well. The robust and hardy soldier, suddenly without tangible cause, felt his strength give way. "It is nothing," his physician said; "a slight attack of fever." Vespasian shook his head; he knew things of which the physician was ignorant. "It is death," he answered, "and an emperor should meet it standing."

Titus' turn came next. A violent, headstrong, handsome, rapacious prince, terribly prodigal, thoroughly Oriental, surrounded by dancers and mignons, living in state with a queen for mistress, startling even Rome with the uproar of his debauches--no sooner was Vespasian gone than presto! the queen went home, the dancers disappeared, the debauches ceased, and a ruler appeared who declared he had lost a day that a good action had not marked; a ruler who could announce that no one should leave his presence depressed.

Though Vespasian had gone, his reign continued. Not long, it is true, and punctuated by a spectacle of which Caligula, for all his poetry, had not dreamed--the burial of Pompeii. But a reign which, while it lasted, was fastidious and refined, and during which, again and again, Titus, who commanded death and whom death obeyed, besought Domitian to be to him a brother.

Domitian had no such intention. He had a party behind him, one made up of old Neronians, the army of the discontented, who wanted a change, and greatly admired this charming young prince whose hours were passed in killing flies and making love to married women. The pretorians too had been seduced. Domitian could make captivating promises when he chose.

As a consequence Titus, like Vespasian, was uneasy, and with cause. Dion Cassius, or rather that brute Xiphilin, his abbreviator, mentions the fever that overtook him, the same his father had met. It was mortal, of course, and the purple was Domitian's.

For a year and a day thereafter you would have thought Titus still at the helm. There was the same clemency, the same regard for justice, the same refinement and fastidiousness. The morose young poet had developed into a model monarch. The old Neronians were perplexed, irritated too; they had expected other things. Domitian was merely feeling the way; the hand that held the sceptre was not quite sure of its strength, and, tentatively almost, this Prince of Virtue began to scrutinize the morals of Rome. For the first time he noticed that the cocottes took their airing in litters. But litters were not for them! That abuse he put a stop to at once. A senator manifested an interest in ballet-girls; he was disgraced. The vestals, to whose indiscretions no one had paid much attention, learned the statutes of an archaic law, and were buried alive. The early distaste for blood was diminishing. Domitian had the purple, but it was not bright enough; he wanted it red, and what Domitian wanted he got. Your god and master orders it, was the formula he began to use when addressing the Senate and People of Rome.

To that the people were indifferent. The spectacles he gave in the Flavian amphitheatre were too magnificently atrocious not to be a compensation in full for any eccentricity in which he might indulge. Besides, under Nero, Claud, Caligula, on en avait vu bien d'autres. And at those spectacles where he presided, crowned with a tiara, on which were the images of Jupiter, Juno and Minerva, while grouped about him the college of Flavian flamens wore tiaras that differed therefrom merely in this, that they bore his image too, the people right royally applauded their master and their god.

And it was just as well they did; Domitian was quite capable of ordering everybody into the arena. As yet, however, he had appeared little different from any other prince. That Rome might understand that there was a difference, and also in what that difference consisted, he gave a supper. Everyone worth knowing was bidden, and, as is usual in state functions, everyone that was bidden came. The supper hall was draped with black; the ceiling, the walls, the floor, everything was basaltic. The couches were black, the linen was black, the slaves were black. Behind each guest was a broken column with his name on it. The food was such as is prepared when death has come. The silence was that of the tomb. The only audible voice was Domitian's. He was talking very wittily and charmingly about murder, about proscriptions, the good informers do, the utility of the headsman, the majesty of the law. The guests, a trifle ill at ease, wished their host sweet dreams. "The same to you," he answered, and deplored that they must go.

On the morrow informers and headsmen were at work. Any pretext was sufficient. Birth, wealth, fame, or the lack of them--anything whatever--and there the culprit stood, charged not with treason to an emperor, but with impiety to a god. On the judgment seat Domitian sat. Before him the accused passed, and under his eyes they were questioned, tortured, condemned and killed. At once their property passed into the keeping of the prince.

Of that he had need. The arena was expensive, but the drain was elsewhere. A little before, a quarrelsome people, the Dacians, whom it took a Trajan to subdue, had overrun the Danube, and were marching down to Rome. Domitian set out to meet them. The Dacians retreated, not at all because they were repulsed, but because Domitian thought it better warfare to pay them to do so. On his return after that victory he enjoyed a triumph as fair as that of Caesar. And each year since then the emperor of Rome had paid tribute to a nation of mongrel oafs.

Of course he needed money. The informers were there and he got it, and with it that spectacle of torture and of blood which he needed too. Curiously, his melancholy increased; his good looks had gone; Psyche was no longer amorous of his eyes. Something else haunted him, something he could not define; the past, perhaps, perhaps the future. To his ears came strange sounds, the murmur of his own name, and suddenly silence. Then, too, there always seemed to be something behind him; something that when he turned disappeared. The room in which he slept he had covered with a polished metal that reflected everything, yet still the intangible was there. Once Pallas came in her chariot, waved him farewell, and disappeared, borne by black horses across the black night.

The astrologers consulted had nothing pleasant to say. They knew, as Domitian knew, that the end was near. So was theirs. To one of them, who predicted his immediate death, he inquired, "What will your end be?" "I," answered the astrologer--"I shall be torn by dogs." "To the stake with him!" cried Domitian; "let him be burned alive!" Suetonius says that a storm put out the flames, and dogs devoured the corpse. Another astrologer predicted that Domitian would die before noon on the morrow. In order to convince him of his error, Domitian ordered him to be executed the subsequent night. Before noon on the morrow Domitian was dead.

Philostratus and Dion Cassius both unite in saying that at that hour Apollonius was at Ephesus, preaching to the multitude. In the middle of the sermon he hesitated, but in a moment he began anew. Again he hesitated, his eyes half closed; then, suddenly he shouted, "Strike him! Strike him once more!" And immediately to his startled audience he related a scene that was occurring at Rome, the attack on Domitian, his struggle with an assailant, his effort to tear out his eyes, the rush of conspirators, and finally the fall of the emperor, pierced by seven knives.

The story may not be true, and yet if it were!

VII
THE POISON IN THE PURPLE

Rome never was healthy. The tramontana visited it then as now, fever, too, and sudden death. To emperors it was fatal. Since Caesar a malaria had battened on them all. Nerva escaped, but only through abdication. The mantle that fell from Domitian's shoulders on to his was so dangerous in its splendor, that, fearing the infection, he passed it to Ulpius Trajanus, the lustre undimmed.

Ulpius Trajanus, Trajan for brevity, a Spaniard by birth, a soldier by choice; one who had fought against Parthian and Jew, who had triumphed through Pannonia and made it his own; a general whose hair had whitened on the field; a consul who had frightened nations, was afraid of the sheen of that purple which dazzled, corroded and killed. He bore it, indeed, but at arm's-length. He kept himself free from the subtlety of its poison, from the microbes of Rome as well.

He was in Cologne when Domitian died and Nerva accepted and renounced the throne. It was a year before he ventured among the seven hills. When he arrived you would have said another Augustus, not the real Augustus, but the Augustus of legend, and the late Mr. Gibbon. When he girt the new prefect of the pretorium with the immemorial sword, he addressed him in copy-book phrases--"If I rule wisely, use it for me; unwisely, against me."

Rome listened open-mouthed. The change from Domitian's formula, "Your god and master orders it," was too abrupt to be immediately understood. Before it was grasped Trajan was off again; this time to the Danube and beyond it, to Dacia and her fens.

Many years later--a century or two, to be exact--a Persian satrap loitered in a forum of Rome. "It is here," he declared, "I am tempted to forget that man is mortal."

He had passed beneath a triumphal arch; before him was a glittering square, grandiose, yet severe; a stretch of temples and basilicas, in which masterpieces felt at home--the Forum of Trajan, the compliment of a nation to a prince. Dominating it was a column, in whose thick spirals you read to-day the one reliable chronicle of the Dacian campaign. Was not Gautier well advised when he said only art endures?

There were other chronicles in plenty; there were the histories of AElius Maurus, of Marius Maximus, and that of Spartian, but they are lost. There is a page or two in the abbreviation which Xiphilin made of Dion; Aurelius Victor has a little to add, so also has Eutropus, but, practically speaking, there is, apart from that column, nothing save conjecture.

Campaigns are wearisome reading, but not the one that is pictured there. You ask a curve a question, and in the next you find the reply. There is a point, however, on which it is dumb--the origin of the war. But if you wish to know the result, not the momentary and transient result, but the sequel which futurity held, look at the ruins at that column's base.

The origin of the war was Domitian's diplomacy. The chieftain whom he had made king, and who had been surprised enough at receiving a diadem instead of the point of a sword, fancied, and not unreasonably, that the annuity which Rome paid him was to continue forever. But Domitian, though a god, was not otherwise immortal. When he died abruptly the annuity ceased. The Dacian king sent word that he was surprised at the delay, but he must have been far more so at the promptness with which he got Trajan's reply. It was a blare of bugles, which he thought forever dumb; a flight of eagles, which he thought were winged.

In the spirals of the column you see the advancing army, the retreating foe; then the Dacian dragon saluting the standards of Rome; peace declared, and an army, whose very repose is menacing, standing there to see that peace is kept. And was it? In the ascending spiral is the new revolt, the attempt to assassinate Trajan, the capture of the conspirators, the advance of the legions, the retreat of the Dacians, burning their cities as they go, carrying their wounded and their women with them, and at last pressing about a huge cauldron that is filled with poison, fighting among themselves for a cup of the brew, and rolling on the ground in the convulsions of death. Farther on is the treasure of the king. To hide it he had turned a river from its source, sunk the gold in a vault beneath, and killed the workmen that had labored there. Beyond is the capture of the capital, the suicide of the chief, a troop of soldiers driving captives and cattle before them, the death of a nation and the end of war.

The subsequent triumph does not appear on the column. It is said that ten thousand beasts were slaughtered in the arenas, slaughtering, as they fell, a thousand of their slaughterers. But the spectacle, however fair, was not of a nature to detain Trajan long in Rome. The air there had not improved in the least, and presently he was off again, this time on the banks of the Euphrates, arguing with the Parthians, avoiding danger in the only way he knew, by facing it.

It was then that the sheen of the purple glowed. If lustreless at home, it was royally red abroad. In a campaign that was little more than a triumphant promenade he doubled the empire. To the world of Caesar he added that of Alexander. Allies he turned into subjects, vassals into slaves. Armenia, Mesopotamia, Assyria, were added to the realm. Trajan's footstools were diadems. He had moved back one frontier, he moved another. From Britain to the Indus, Rome was mistress of the earth. Had Trajan been younger, China, whose very name was unknown, would have yielded to him her corruption, her printing press, her powder and her tea.

That he would have enjoyed these things is not at all conjectural. He was then an old man, but he was not a good one--at least not in the sense we use the term today. He had habits which are regarded now less as vices than perversions, but which at that time were taken as a matter of course and accepted by everyone, even by the stoics, very calmly, with a grain of Attic salt at that. Men were regarded as virtuous when they were brave, when they were honest; the idea of using the expression in its later sense occurred, if at all, in jest merely, as a synonym for the eunuch. It was the matron and the vestal who were supposed to be straight, and their straightness was wholly supposititious. The ceremonies connected with the phallus, and those observed in the worship of the Bona Dea, were of a nature that no virtue could withstand. Every altar, Juvenal said, had its Clodius, and even in Clodius' absence there were always those breaths of Sapphic song that blew through Mitylene.

It is just that absence of a quality which we regard as an added grace; one, parenthetically, which dowered the world with a new conception of beauty that makes it difficult to picture Rome. Modern ink has acquired Nero's blush; it comes very readily, yet, however sensitive a writer may be, once Roman history is before him, he may violate it if he choose; he may even give it a child, but never can he make it immaculate. He may skip, indeed, if he wish; and it is because he has skipped so often that one fancies that Augustus was all right. The rain of fire which fell on the cities that mirrored their towers in the Bitter Sea, might just as well have fallen on him, on Vergil, too, on Caligula, Claud, Nero, Otho, Vitellius, Titus, Domitian, and particularly on Trajan.

As lieutenant in the latter's triumphant promenade, was a nephew, AElius Hadrianus, a young man for whom Trajan's wife is rumored to have had more than a platonic affection, and who in younger days was numbered among Trajan's mignons.

During the progress of that promenade Trajan fell ill. The command of the troops was left to Hadrian, and Trajan started for Rome. On the way he died. In what manner is not known; his wife, however, was with him, and it was in her hand that a letter went to the senate stating that Trajan had adopted Hadrian as his heir. Trajan had done nothing of the sort. The idea had indeed occurred to him, but long since it had been abandoned. He had even formally selected someone else, but his wife was with him, and her lover commanded the troops. The lustre of the purple, always dazzling, had fascinated Hadrian's eyes. Did he steal it? One may conjecture, yet never know. In any event it was his, and he folded it very magnificently about him. Still young, a trifle over thirty, handsome, unusually accomplished, grand seigneur to his finger-tips, endowed with a manner which is rumored to have been one of great charm, possessed of the amplest appreciation of the elegancies of life, he had precisely the figure which purple adorns. But, though the lustre had fascinated, he too knew its spell; and presently he started off on a journey about the world, which lasted fifteen years, and which, when ended, left the world the richer for his passing, decorated with the monuments he had strewn. Before that journey began, at the earliest rumor of Trajan's death, the Euphrates and Tigris awoke, the cinders of Nineveh flamed. The rivers and land that lay between knew that their conqueror had gone. Hadrian knew it also, and knew too that, though he might occupy the warrior's throne, he never could fill the warrior's place. To Armenia, Mesopotamia, Assyria, freedom was restored. Dacia could have had it for the asking. But over Dacia the toga had been thrown; it was as Roman as Gaul. A corner of it is Roman still; the Roumanians are there. But though Dacia was quiet, in its neighborhood the restless Sarmatians prowled and threatened. Hadrian, who had already written a book on tactics, knew at once how to act. Domitian's policy was before him; he followed the precedent, and paid the Sarmatians to be still. It requires little acumen to see that when Rome permitted herself to be blackmailed the end was near.

For the time being, however, there was peace, and in its interest Hadrian set out on that unequalled journey over a land that was his. Had fate relented, Trajan could have made a wider one still. But in Trajan was the soldier merely, when he journeyed it was with the sword. In Hadrian was the dilettante, the erudite too; he travelled not to conquer, but to learn, to satisfy an insatiable curiosity, for self-improvement, for glory too. Behind him was an army, not of soldiers, but of masons, captained by architects, artists and engineers. Did a site please him, there was a temple at once, or if not that, then a bridge, an aqueduct, a library, a new fashion, sovereignty even, but everywhere the spectacle of an emperor in flesh and blood. For the first time the provinces were able to understand that a Caesar was not necessarily a brute, a phantom and a god.

It would have been interesting to have made one of that court of poets and savants that surrounded him; to have dined with him in Paris, eaten oysters in London; sat with him while he watched that wall go up before the Scots, and then to have passed down again through a world still young--a world beautiful, ornate, unutilitarian; a world to which trams, advertisements and telegraph poles had not yet come; a world that still had illusions, myths and mysteries; one in which religion and poetry went hand in hand--a world without newspapers, hypocrisy and cant.

Hadrian, doubtless, enjoyed it. He was young enough to have enthusiasms and to show them; he was one of the best read men of the day; he was poet, painter, sculptor, musician, erudite and emperor in one. Of course he enjoyed it. The world, over which he travelled, was his, not by virtue of the purple alone, but because of his knowledge of it. The prince is not necessarily cosmopolitan; the historian and antiquarian are. Hadrian was an early Quinet, an earlier Champollion; always the thinker, sometimes the cook. And to those in his suite it must have been a sight very unique to see a Caesar who had published his volume of erotic verse, just as any other young man might do; who had hunted lions, not in the arena, but in Africa, make researches on the plain where Troy had been, and a supreme of sow's breast, peacock, pheasant, ham and boar, which he called Pentapharmarch, and which he offered as he had his Catacriani--the erotic verse--as something original and nice.

Insatiably inquisitive, verifying a history that he was preparing in the lands which gave that history birth, he passed through Egypt and Asia, questioning sphinxes, the cerements of kings, the arcana of the temples; deciphering the sacred books, arguing with magi, interrogating the stars. For the thinker, after the fashion of the hour, was astrologer too, and one of the few anecdotes current concerning him is in regard to a habit he had of drawing up on the 31st of December the events of the coming year. After consulting the stars on that 31st of December which occurred in the twenty-second year of his reign, he prepared a calendar which extended only to the 10th of July. On that day he died.

The calendar does not seem to have been otherwise serviceable. It was in Bithynia he found a shepherd whose appearance which, in its perfection, was quite earthly, suggested neither heaven nor hell, but some planet where the atmosphere differs from ours; where it is pink, perhaps, or faintly ochre; where birth and death have forms higher than here.

Hadrian, captivated, led the lad in leash. The facts concerning that episode have been so frequently given that the repetition is needless here. Besides, the point is elsewhere. Presently the lad fell overboard. Hadrian lost a valet, Rome an emperor, and Olympus a god. But in attempting to deify the lost lackey, the grief of Hadrian was so immediate, that it is permissible to fancy that the lad's death was not one of those events which the emperor-astrologer noted beforehand on his calendar. The lad was decently buried, the Nile gave up her dead, and on the banks a fair city rose, one that had its temples, priests, altars and shrines; a city that worshipped a star, and called that star Antinous. Hadrian then could have congratulated himself. Even Caligula would have envied him. He had done his worst; he had deified not a lad, but a lust. And not for the moment alone. A half century later Tertullian noted that the worship still endured, and subsequently the Alexandrine Clement discovered consciences that Antinous had reproached.

Antinous, deified, was presently forgot. A young Roman, wonderfully beautiful, Dion says, yet singularly effeminate; a youth who could barely carry a shield; who slept between rose-leaves and lilies; who was an artist withal; a poet who had written lines that Martial might have mistaken for his own, Cejonius Verus by name, succeeded the Bithynian shepherd. Hadrian, who would have adopted Antinous, adopted Verus in his stead. But Hadrian was not happy in his choice. Verus died, and singularly enough, Hadrian selected as future emperor the one ruler against whom history has not a reproach, Pius Antonin.

Meanwhile the journey continued. The Thousand and One Nights were realized then if ever. The beauty of the world was at its apogee, the glory of Rome as well; and through secrets and marvels Hadrian strolled, note-book in hand, his eyes unwearied, his curiosity unsatiated still. To pleasure him the intervales took on a fairer glow; cities decked themselves anew, the temples unveiled their mysteries; and when he passed to the intervales liberty came; to the cities, sovereignty; to the temples, shrines. The world rose to him as a woman greets her lover. His travels were not fatigues; they were delights, in which nations participated, and of which the memories endure as though enchanted still.

It would have been interesting, no doubt, to have dined with him in Paris; to have quarried lions in their African fens; to have heard archaic hymns ripple through the rushes of the Nile; to have lounged in the Academe, to have scaled Parnassus, and sailed the AEgean Sea; but, a history and an arm-chair aiding, the traveller has but to close his eyes and the past returns. Without disturbing so much as a shirt-box, he may repeat that promenade. Triremes have foundered; litters are out of date; painted elephants are no more; the sky has changed, climates with it; there are colors, as there are arts, that have gone from us forever; there are desolate plains, where green and yellow was; the shriek of steam where gods have strayed; advertisements in sacred groves; Baedekers in ruins that never heard an atheist's voice; solitudes where there were splendors; the snarl of jackals where once were birds and bees--yet, history and the arm-chair aiding, it all returns. Any travel-ler may follow in Hadrian's steps; he is stayed but once--on the threshold of the Temple of Eleusis. It is there history gropes, impotent and blind, and it is there the interest of that journey culminated.

Beyond the episode connected with Antinous, Hadrian's journey was marked by another, one which occurred in Judaea. Both were infamous, no doubt, but, what is more to the point, both mark the working of the poison in the purple that he bore.

Since Titus had gone, despairful Judaea had taken heart again. Hope in that land was inextinguishable. The walls of Jerusalem were still standing; in the Temple the offices continued. Though Rome remained, there was Israel too. Passing that way one afternoon, Hadrian mused. The city affected him; the site was superb. And as he mused it occurred to him that Jerusalem was less harmonious to the ear than Hadrianopolis; that the Temple occupied a position on which a Capitol would look far better; in brief, that Jehovah might be advantageously replaced by Jove. The army of masons that were ever at his heels were set to work at once. They had re-ceived similar orders and performed similar tasks so often that they could not fancy anyone would object. The Jews did. They fought as they had never fought before; they fought for three years against a Nebuchadnezzar who created torrents of blood so abundant that stones were carried for miles, and who left corpses enough to fertilize the land for a decade. The survivors were sold. Those for whom no purchasers could be found had their heads amputated. Jerusalem was razed to the ground. The site of the Temple was furrowed by the plow, sown with salt, and in place of the City of David rose AElia Capitolina, a miniature Rome, whose gates, save on one day in the year, Jews were forbidden under penalty of death to pass, were forbidden to look at, and over which were images of swine, pigs with scornful snouts, the feet turned inward, the tail twisted like a lie.

It was not honorable warfare, but it was effective; then, too, it was Hadrianesque, the mad insult of a madman to a race as mad as he. The purple had done its work. History has left the rise of this emperor conjectural; his fall is written in blood. As he began he ended, a poet and a beast.

Presently he was in Rome. It was not homesickness that took him there; he was far too cosmopolitan to suffer from any such malady as that. It was the accumulations of a fifteen-year excursion through the metropoles of art which demanded a gallery of their own. Another with similar tastes and similar power might have ordered everything which pleasured his eye to be carted to Rome, but in his quality of artifex omnipotens Hadrian embellished and never sacked. There were painters and sculptors enough in that army at his heels, and whatever appealed to him was copied on the spot. So much was copied that a park of ten square miles was just large enough to form the open-air museum which he had designed, one which centuries of excavation have not exhausted yet.

The museum became a mad-house. Hadrian was ill; tired in mind and body, smitten with imperialia. It was then the young Verus died, leaving for a wonder a child behind, and more wonderful still, Antonin was adopted. Through Rome, meanwhile, terror stalked. Hadrian, in search of a remedy against his increasing confusion of mind, his visible weakness of body, turned from physicians to oracles; from them to magic, and then to blood. He decimated the senate. Soldiers, freemen, citizens, anybody and everybody were ordered off to death. He tried to kill himself and failed; he tried again, wondering, no doubt, why he who commanded death for others could not command it for himself. Presently he succeeded, and Antonin-- the pious Antonin, as the senate called him--marshalled from cellars and crypts the senators and citizens whom Hadrian had ordered to be destroyed.

VIII
FAUSTINE

Anyone who has loitered a moment among the statues in the Salle des Antonins at the Louvre will recall the bust of the Empress Faustina. It stands near the
entrance, coercing the idler to remove his hat; to stop a moment, to gaze and dream.
The face differs from that which Mr. Swinburne has described. In the poise of the
head, in the expression of the lips, particularly in the features which, save the low
brow, are not of the Roman type, there is a commingling of just that loveliness and
melancholy which must have come to Psyche when she lost her god. In the corners
of the mouth, in the droop of the eyelids, in the moulding of the chin, you may see
that rarity--beauty and intellect in one--and with it the heightening shadow of an
eternal regret. Before her Marcus Aurelius, her husband, stands, decked with the
purple, with all the splendor of the imperator, his beard in overlapping curls, his
questioning eyes dilated. Beyond is her daughter, Lucille, less fair than the mother,
a healthy girl of the dairymaid type. Near by is the son, Commodus. Across the hall
is Lucius Verus, the husband of Lucille; in a corner, Antonin, Faustine's father, and,
more remotely, his wife. Together they form quite a family group, and to the aver-
age tourist they must seem a thoroughly respectable lot. Antonin certainly was respectable. He was the first emperor who declined to be a brute. Referring to his wife
he said that he would rather be with her in a desert than without her in a palace; the
speech, parenthetically, of a man who, though he could have cited that little Greek
princess, Nausicaa, as a precedent, was too well-bred to permit so much as a fringe
of his household linen to flutter in public. Besides, at his hours, he was a poet, and it
is said that if a poet tell a lie twice he will believe it. Antonin so often declared his
wife to be a charming person that in the end no doubt he thought so. She was not
charming, however, or if she were, her charm was not that of exclusiveness.

It was in full sight of this lady's inconsequences that Faustine was educated.
Wherever she looked, the candors of her girlhood were violated. The phallus then
was omnipresent. Iamblicus, not the novelist, but the philosopher, has much to
say on the subject; as has Arnobius in the Adversus gentes, and Lactance in the De

falsa religione. If Juvenal, Martial, Petronius, are more reticent, it is because they were not Fathers of the Church, nor yet antiquarians. No one among us exacts a description of a spire. The phallus was as common to them, commoner even. It was on the coins, on the doors, in the gardens. As a preservative against Envy it hung from children's necks. On sun-dials and water clocks it marked the flight of time. The vestals worshipped it. At weddings it was used in a manner which need not be described.

It was from such surroundings that Faustine stepped into the arms of the severe and stately prince whom her father had chosen. That Marcus Aurelius adored her is certain. His notebook shows it. A more tender-hearted and perfect lover romance may show, but history cannot. He must have been the quintessence of refinement, a thoroughbred to his finger-tips; one for whom that purple mantle was too gaudy, and yet who bore it, as he bore everything else, in that self-abnegatory spirit which the higher reaches of philosophy bring.

He was of that rare type that never complains and always consoles.

After Antonin's death, his hours ceased to be his own. On the Euphrates there was the wildest disorder. To the north new races were pushing nations over the Danube and the Rhine. From the catacombs Christ was emerging; from the Nile, Serapis. The empire was in disarray. Antonin had provided his son-in-law with a coadjutor, Lucius Verus, the son of Hadrian's mignon, a magnificent scoundrel; a tall, broad-shouldered athlete, with a skin as fresh as a girl's and thick curly hair, which he covered with a powder of gold; a viveur, whose suppers are famous still; whose guests were given the slaves that served them, the plate off which they had eaten, the cups from which they had drunk--cups of gold, cups of silver, jewelled cups, cups from Alexandria, murrhine vases filled with nard--cars and litters to go home with, mules with silver trappings and negro muleteers. Capitolinus says that, while the guests feasted, sometimes the magnificent Verus got drunk, and was carried to bed in a coverlid, or else, the red feather aiding, turned out and fought the watch.

It was this splendid individual to whom Marcus Aurelius entrusted the Euphrates. They had been brought up together, sharing each others tutors, writing themes for the same instructor, both meanwhile adolescently enamored of the fair Faustine. It was to Marcus she was given, the empire as a dower; and when that dower passed into his hands, he could think of nothing more equitable than to ask Verus to share it with him. Verus was not stupid enough to refuse, and at the hour when the Parthians turned ugly, he needed little urging to set out for the East, dreaming, as he did so, of creating there an empire that should be wholly his.

At that time Faustine must have been at least twenty-eight, possibly thirty. There were matrons who had not seen their fifteenth year, and Faustine had been married young. Her daughter, Lucille, was nubile. Presently Verus, or rather his lieutenants, succeeded, and the girl was betrothed to him. There was a festival, of course, games in abundance, and plenty of blood.

It would have been interesting to have seen her that day, the iron ring of betrothal on her finger, her brother, Commodus, staring at the arrangement of her hair, her mother prettily perplexed, her father signing orders which messengers brought and despatched while the sand took on a deeper red, and Rome shrieked its delight. Yes, it would have been interesting and typical of the hour. Her hair in the ten tresses which were symbolic of a fiancee's innocence, must have amused that brute of a brother of hers, and the iron ring on the fourth finger of her left hand must have given Faustine food for thought; the vestals, in their immaculate robes, must have gazed at her in curious, sisterly ways, and because of her fresh beauty surely there were undertones of applause. Should her father disappear she would make a gracious imperatrix indeed.

But, meanwhile, there was Faustine, and at sight of her legends of old imperial days returned. She was not Messalina yet, but in the stables there were jockeys whose sudden wealth surprised no one; in the arenas there were gladiators that fought, not for liberty, nor for death, but for the caresses of her eyes; in the side-scenes there were mimes who spoke of her; there were senators who boasted in their cups, and in the theatre Rome laughed colossally at the catchword of her amours.

Marcus Aurelius then was occupied with affairs of state. In similar circumstances so was Claud--Messalina's husband--so, too, was Antonin. But Claud was an imbecile, Antonin a man of the world, while Marcus Aurelius was a philosopher. When fate links a woman to any one of these varieties of the husband, she is blessed indeed. Faustine was particularly favored.

The stately prince was not alone a philosopher--a calling, by the way, which was common enough then, and has become commoner since--he was a philosopher who believed in philosophy, a rarity then as now. The exact trend of his thought is difficult to define. His note-book is filled with hesitations; materialism had its allurements, so also had pantheism; the advantages of the Pyrrhonic suspension of judgment were clear to him too; according to the frame of mind in which he wrote, you might fancy him an agnostic, again an akosmist, sometimes both, but always the ethical result is the same.

"Revenge yourself on your enemy by not resembling him. Forgive; forgive always; die forgiving. Be indulgent to the wrong-doer; be compassionate to him; tell him how he should act; speak to him without anger, without sarcasm; speak to him affectionately. Besides, what do you know of his wrong-doing? Are all his thoughts familiar to you? May there not be something that justifies him? And you, are you entirely free from reproach? Have you never done wrong? And if not, was it fear that restrained you? Was it pride, or what?"

In the synoptic gospels similar recommendations appear. Charity is the New Testament told in a word. Christians read and forget it. But Christians are not philosophers. The latter are charitable because they regard evil as a part of the universal order of things, one which it is idle to blame, yet permissible to rectify.

From whatever source such a tenet springs, whether from materialism, stoicism, pyrrhonism, epicureanism, atheism even, is of small matter; it is a tenet which is honorable to the holder. This sceptred misanthrope possessed it, and it was in that his wife was blessed. Years later he died, forgiving her in silence, praising her aloud. Claud, referring to Messalina, shouted through the Forum that the fate which destined him to marry impure women destined him to punish them. Marcus Aurelius said nothing. He did not know what fate destined him to do, but he did know that philosophy taught him to forgive.

It was this philosophy that first perplexed Faustine. She was restless, frivolous, perhaps also a trifle depraved. Frivolous because all women were, depraved because her mother was, and restless because of the curiosity that inflammable imaginations share--in brief, a Roman princess. Her husband differed from the Roman prince. His youth had not been entirely circumspect; he, too, had his curiosities, but they were satisfied, he had found that they stained. When he married he was already the thinker; doubtless, he was tiresome; he could have had little small-talk, and his hours of love-making must have been rare. Presently the affairs of state engrossed him. Faustine was left to herself; save a friend of her own sex, a woman can have no worse companion. She, too, discovered she had curiosities. A gladiator passed that way--then Rome; then Lesbos; then the Lampsacene. "You are my husband's mistress," her daughter cried at her. "And you," the mother answered, "are your brother's." Even in the aridity of a chronicle the accusation and rejoinder are dramatic. Fancy what they must have been when mother and daughter hissed them in each other's teeth. Whether the argument continued is immaterial. Both could have claimed the sanction of religion. In those days a sin was a prayer. Religion was then, as it always had been, purely political. With the individual, with his happiness or aspirations, it concerned itself not at all. It was the prosperity of the empire, its peace and immortality, for which sacrifices were made, and libations offered. The god of Rome was Rome, and religion was patriotism. The antique virtues, courage in war, moderation in peace, and honor at all times, were civic, not personal. It was the state that had a soul, not the individual. Man was ephemeral; it was the nation that endured. It was the permanence of its grandeur that was important, nothing else.

To ensure that permanence each citizen labored. As for the citizen, death was near, and he hastened to live; before the roses could fade he wreathed himself with them. Immortality to him was in his descendants, the continuation of his name, respect to his ashes. Any other form of future life was a speculation, infrequent at that. In anterior epochs Fright had peopled Tartarus, but Fright had gone. The Elysian Fields were vague, wearisome to contemplate; even metempsychosis had no adherents. "After death," said Caesar, "there is nothing," and all the world agreed with him. The hour, too, in which three thousand gods had not a single atheist, had gone, never to return. Old faiths had crumbled. None the less was Rome the abridgment of every superstition. The gods of the conquered had always been part of her spoils. The Pantheon had become a lupanar of divinities that presided over birth, and whose rites were obscene; an abattoir of gods that presided over death, and whose worship was gore. To please them was easy. Blood and debauchery was all that was required. That the upper classes had no faith in them at all goes without the need of telling; the atmosphere of their atriums dripped with metaphysics. But of the atheism of the upper classes the people knew nothing; they clung piously to a faith which held a theological justification of every sin, and in the temples fervent prayers were murmured, not for future happiness, for that was unobtainable, nor yet for wisdom or virtue, for those things the gods neither granted nor possessed; the prayers were that the gods would favor the suppliant in his hatreds and in his lusts.

Such was Rome when Verus returned to wed Lucille. Before his car the phallus swung; behind it was the pest. A little before, the Tiber overflowed. Presently, in addition to the pest, famine came. It was patent to everyone that the gods were vexed. There was blasphemy somewhere, and the Christians were tossed to the beasts. Faustine watched them die. At first they were to her as other criminals, but immediately a difference was discerned. They met death, not with grace, perhaps, but with exaltation. They entered the arena as though it were an enchanted garden, the color of the emerald, where dreams came true. Faustine questioned. They were enemies of state, she was told. The reply left her perplexed, and she questioned again. It was then her eyes became inhabited by regret. The past she tried to put from her, but remorse is physical; it declines to be dismissed. She would have killed herself, but she no longer dared. Besides, in the future there was light. In some ray of it she must have walked, for when at the foot of Mount Taurus, in a little Cappadocian village, years later, she died, it was at the sign of the cross.

IX
THE AGONY

The high virtues are not complaisant, it is the cad the canaille adore. In spite of everything, Nero had been beloved by the masses. For years there were roses on his tomb. Under Vespasian there was an impostor whom Greece and Asia acclaimed in his name. The memory of his festivals was unforgetable; regret for him refused to be stilled. He was more than a god; he was a tradition. His second advent was confidently expected; the Jews believed in his resurrection; to the Christian he had never died, and suddenly he reappeared.

Rome had declined to accept the old world tenet that the soul has its avatars, yet, when Commodus sauntered from that distant sepulchre, into which, poison aiding, he had placed his putative father, Rome felt that the Egyptians were wiser than they looked; that the soul did migrate, and that in the blue eyes of the young emperor Nero's spirit shone.

Herodian, who has written very agreeably on the subject, describes him as another Prince Charming. His hair, which was very fair, glistened like gold in the sun; he was slender, not at all effeminate, exceedingly graceful, exceedingly gracious; endowed with the promptest blush, with the best intentions; studious of the interests of his people; glad of advice, seeking it even; courteous and deferential to the senate and his father's friends--in short, an adolescent Nero--a trifle more guileful, however; already a parricide, a comedian as well; one who in a moment would toss the mask aside and disclose the mongrel; the offspring, not of an empress and an emperor, but the tiger-cub that Faustine had got by a gladiator.

The tender-hearted philosopher, who in a campaign against some fretful Teutons, had taken Commodus with him, knew that he was not his son; knew, too, when the agony seized him, from whose hand the agony came; but in earlier life he had jotted in his notebook, "Forgive, forgive always; die forgiving"; and, as he forgave the mother, so he forgave the child, recommending him with his last breath to the army and to Rome.

As the people had loved Nero, so did the aristocracy love Marcus Aurelius; his foster-father Antonin excepted, he was the only gentleman that had sat on the throne. No wonder they loved him; and seeing this early edition of the prince in the fairy tale emerge from the bogs of Germany, his fair face haloed by the glisten and gold of his hair, hearts went out to him; the wish of his putative father was ratified, and the son of a gladiator was emperor of Rome.

Lampridus--or Spartian was it? The title-page bears Lampridus' name, but there is some doubt as to the authorship. However, whoever made the abridgment of the life of Commodus which appears among the chronicles of the Scriptores Historiae Augustae, says that before his birth Faustine dreamed she had engendered a serpent. It is not impossible that Faustine had been reading Ctzias, and had stumbled over his account of the Martichoras, a serpent with a woman's face and the talons of a bird of prey. For it was that she conceived.

It would have been interesting to have seen that young man, the mask removed, frightening the senate into calling Rome Commodia, and then in a linen robe promenading in the attributes of a priest of Anubis through a seraglio of six hundred girls and mignons embracing as he passed. There was a spectacle, which Nero had not imagined. But Nero was vieux jeu. Commodus outdid him, first in debauchery, then in the arena. Nero had died while in training to kill a lion; Commodus did not take the trouble to train. It was the lions that were trained, not he. A skin on his shoulders, a club in his hand, he descended naked into the ring, and there felled beasts and men. Then, acclaimed as Hercules, he returned to the pulvina, and a mignon on one side, a mistress on the other, ordered the guard to massacre the spectators and set fire to Rome. After entering the arena six or seven hundred times, and there vanquishing men whose eyes had been put out and whose legs were tied, the colossal statue which Nero had made after his own image was altered; to the top came the bust of Commodus, to the base this legend: THE VICTOR OF TEN THOUSAND GLADIATORS, COMMODUS-HERCULES, IMPERATOR.

Meanwhile conspirators were at work. Like Nero, Commodus could have sought in vain for a friend. His life was attempted again and again; he escaped, but never the plotters; only when they had gone there were more. He knew he was doomed. There was the usual comet; the statue of Hercules had perspired visibly; an owl had been caught above his bedroom, and once he had wiped in his hair the hand which he had plunged in the warm wound of a gladiator, dead at his feet. These omens could mean but one thing. None the less, if he were doomed, so were others. One day one of those miserable children that the emperors kept about them found a tablet. It was as good as anything else to play with; and, as the child tossed it through the hall, the one woman that had loved Commodus caught it and read on it that she and all the household were to die. Within an hour Commodus was killed.

There is a page in Lampridus, which he quotes as coming from the lost chronicles of Marius Maximus, and which contains the joy of the senate at the news. It is too long for transcription, but as a bit of realism it is unique. There is a shiver in every line. You hear the voices of hundreds, drunk with fury, frenzied with delight; the fierce welcome that greeted Pertinax--a slave's grandson, who was emperor for a minute--the joy of hate assuaged.

The delight of the senate was not shared by the pretorians. Pertinax was promptly massacred; the throne was put up at auction; there were two or three emperors at once, and presently the purple was seized by Septimus Severus, a rigid, white-haired disciplinarian, who, in his admiration for Marcus Aurelius, founded that second dynasty of the Antonins with which antiquity may be said to end.

When he had gone, his elder son, Bastian, renamed Aurelius Antonin, and because of a cloak he had invented nicknamed Caracalla, bounded like a panther on the throne. In a moment he was gnawing at his brother's throat, and immediately there occurred a massacre such as Rome had never seen. Xiphilin says the nights were not long enough to kill all of the condemned. Twenty thousand people were slaughtered in twenty hours. The streets were emptied, the theatres closed.

The blood that ran then must have been in rillets too thin to slake Caracalla's thirst, for simultaneously almost, he was in Gaul, in Dacia--wherever there was prey. African by his father, Syrian on his mother's side, Caracalla was not a panther merely; he was a herd of them. He had the cruelty, the treachery and guile of a wilderness of tiger-cats. No man, said a thinker, is wholly base. Caracalla was. He had not a taste, not a vice, even, which was not washed and rewashed in blood. In a moment of excitement Commodus set his guards on the spectators in the amphitheatre; the damage was slight, for the Colosseum was so constructed that in two minutes the eighty or ninety thousand people which it held could escape. Caracalla had the exits closed. Those who escaped were naked; to bribe the guards they were forced to strip themselves to the skin. In the circus a vestal caught his eye. He tried to violate her, and failing impotently, had her buried alive. "Caracalla knows that I am a virgin, and knows why," the girl cried as the earth swallowed her, but there was no one there to aid.

Such things show the trend of a temperament, though not, perhaps, its force. Presently the latter was displayed. For years those arch-enemies of Rome, the unconquerable Parthians, had been quiet; bound, too, by treaties which held Rome's honor. Not Caracalla's, however; he had none. An embassy went out to Artobane, the king. Caracalla wished a bride, and what fairer one could he have than the child of the Parthian monarch? Then, too, the embassy was charged to explain, the marriage of Rome and Parthia would be the union of the Orient and the Occident, peace by land and sea. Artobane hesitated, and with cause; but Caracalla wooed so ardently that finally the king said yes. The news went abroad. The Parthians, delighted, prepared to receive the emperor. When Caracalla crossed the Tigris, the highroad that led to the capital was strewn with sacrifices, with altars covered with flowers, with welcomings of every kind. Caracalla was visibly pleased. Beyond the gates of the capital, there was the king; he had advanced to greet his son-in-law, and that the greeting might be effective, he had assembled his nobles and his troops. The latter were armed with cymbals, with hautbois, and with flutes; and as Caracalla and his army approached, there was music, dancing and song; there were libations too, and as the day was practically the wedding of East and West, there was not a weapon to be seen--gala robes merely, brilliant and long. Caracalla saluted the king, gave an order to an adjutant, and on the smiling defenceless Parthians the Roman eagles pounced. Those who were not killed were made prisoners of war. The next day Caracalla withdrew, charged with booty, firing cities as he went.

A little before, rumor reached him that a group of the citizens of Alexandria had referred to him as a fratricide. After the adventure in Parthia he bethought him of the city which Alexander had founded, and of the temple of Serapis that was there. He wished to honor both, he declared, and presently he was at the gates. The people were enchanted; the avenues were strewn with flowers, lined with musicians. There were illuminations, festivals, sacrifices, torrents of perfumes, and through it all Caracalla passed, a legion at his heels. To see him, to participate in the succession of prodigalities, the surrounding country flocked there too. In recognition of the courtesy with which he was received, Caracalla gave a banquet to the magnates and the clergy. Before his guests could leave him they were killed. Through the streets the legion was at work. Alexandria was turned into a cemetery. Herodian states that the carnage was so great that the Nile was red to its mouth.

In Rome at that time was a prefect, Macrin by name, who had dreamed the purple would be his. He was a swarthy liar, and his promises were such that the pretorians were willing that the dream should come true. Emissaries were despatched, and Caracalla was stabbed. In his luggage poison was found to the value of five million five hundred thousand drachmae. What fresh turpitude he was devising no one knew, and the discovery might serve as an epitaph, were it not that by his legions he was adored. No one had abandoned to the army such booty as he.

Meanwhile, in a chapel at Emissa, a boy was dancing indolently to the kiss of flutes. A handful of Caracalla's soldiers passed that way, and thought him Bacchus. In his face was the enigmatic beauty of gods and girls--the charm of the dissolute and the wayward heightened by the divine. On his head was a diadem; his frail tunic was of purple and gold, but the sleeves, after the Phoenician fashion, were wide, and he was shod with a thin white leather that reached to the thighs. He was fourteen, and priest of the Sun. The chapel was roomy and rich. There was no statue--a black phallus merely, which had fallen from above, and on which, if you looked closely, you could see the image of Elagabal, the Sun.

The rumor of his beauty brought other soldiers that way, and the lad, feeling that Rome was there, ceased to dance, strolling through pauses of the worship, a troop of galli at his heels, surveying the intruders with querulous, feminine eyes.

Presently a whisper filtered that the lad was Caracalla's son. There were centurions there that remembered Semiamire, the lad's mother, very well; they had often seen her, a superb creature with scorching eyes, before whom fire had been carried as though she were empress. It was she who had put it beyond Caracalla's power to violate that vestal when he tried. She was his cousin; her life had been passed at court; it was Macrin who had exiled her. And with the whisper filtered another--that she was rich; that she had lumps of gold, which she would give gladly to whomso aided in placing her Antonin on the throne. There were gossips who said ill-natured things of this lady; who insinuated that she had so many lovers that she herself could not tell who was the father of her child; but the lumps of gold had a language of their own. The disbanded army espoused the young priest's cause; there was a skirmish, Macrin was killed, and Heliogabalus was emperor of Rome.

"I would never have written the life of this Antonin Impurissimus," said Lampridus, "were it not that he had predecessors." Even in Latin the task was difficult. In English it is impossible. There are subjects that permit of a hint, particularly if it be masked to the teeth, but there are others that no art can drape. "The inexpressible does not exist," Gautier remarked, when he finished a notorious romance, nor does it; but even his pen would have balked had he tried it on Heliogabalus.

In his work on the Caesars, Suetonius drew breath but once--he called Nero a monster. Subsequently he must have regretted having done so, not because Nero was not a monster, but because it was sufficient to display the beast without adding a descriptive placard. In that was Suetonius' advantage; he could describe. Nowadays a writer may not, or at least not Heliogabalus. It is not merely that he was depraved, for all of that lot were; it was that he made depravity a pursuit; and, the purple favoring, carried it not only beyond the limits of the imaginable, but beyond the limits of the real. At the feet of that painted boy, Elephantis and Parrhasius could have sat and learned a lesson. Apart from that phase of his sovereignty, he was a little Sardanapalus, an Asiatic mignon, who found himself great.

It would have been curious to have seen him in that wonderful palace, clothed like a Persian queen, insisting that he should be addressed as Imperatrix, and quite living up to the title. It would not only be interesting, it would give one an insight into just how much the Romans could stand. It would have been curious, also, to have assisted at that superb and poetic ceremonial, in which, having got Tanit from Carthage as consort for Elagabal, he presided, girt with the pomp of church and state, over the nuptials of the Sun and Moon.

He had read Suetonius, and not an eccentricity of the Caesars escaped him. He would not hunt flies by the hour, as Domitian had done, for that would be mere imitation; but he could collect cobwebs, and he did, by the ton. Caligula and Vitellius had been famous as hosts, but the feasts that Heliogabalus gave outranked them for sheer splendor. From panels in the ceiling such masses of flowers fell that guests were smothered. Those that survived had set before them glass game and sweets of crystal. The menu was embroidered on the table-cloth--not the mere list of dishes, but pictures drawn with the needle of the dishes themselves. And presently, after the little jest in glass had been enjoyed, you were served with camel's heels; combs torn from living cocks; platters of nightingale tongues; ostrich brains, prepared with that garum sauce which the Sybarites invented, and of which the secret is lost; therewith were peas and grains of gold; beans and amber peppered with pearl dust; lentils and rubies; spiders in jelly; lion's dung, served in pastry. The guests that wine overcame were carried to bedrooms. When they awoke, there staring at them were tigers and leopards--tame, of course; but some of the guests were stupid enough not to know it, and died of fright.

All this was of a nature to amuse a lad who had made the phallus the chief object of worship; who had banished Jupiter, dismissed Isis; who, over paths that were strewn with lilies, had himself, in the attributes of Bacchus, drawn by tigers; by lions as Mother of the Gods; again, by naked women, as Heliogabalus on his way to wed a vestal, and procure for the empire a child that should be wholly divine.

It amused Rome, too, and his prodigalities in the circus were such that Lampridus admits that the people were glad he was emperor. Neither Caligula nor Nero had been as lavish, and neither Caligula nor Nero as cruel. The atrocities he committed, if less vast than those of Caracalla's, were more acute. Domitian even was surpassed in the tortures invented by a boy, so dainty that he never used the same garments, the same shoes, the same jewels, the same woman twice.

In spite of this, or perhaps precisely on that account, the usual conspirators were at work, and one day this little painted girl, who had prepared several devices for a unique and splendid suicide, was taken unawares and tossed in the latrinae.

In him the glow of the purple reached its apogee. Rome had been watching a crescendo that had mounted with the years. Its culmination was in that hermaphrodite. But the tension had been too great--something snapped; there was nothing left--a procession of colorless bandits merely, Thracians, Gauls, Pannonians, Dalmatians, Goths, women even, with Attila for a climax and the refurbishing of the world.

Rome was still mistress, but she was growing very old. She had conquered step by step. When one nation had fallen, she garrotted another. To vanquish her, the earth had to produce not only new races, but new creeds. The parturitions, as we know, were successful. Already the blue, victorious eyes of Vandal and of Goth were peering down at Rome; already they had whispered together, and over the hydromel had drunk to her fall. The earth's new children fell upon her, not one by one, but all at once, and presently the colossus tottered, startling the universe with the uproar of her agony; calling to gods that had vacated the skies; calling to Jupiter; calling to Isis; calling in vain. Where the thunderbolt had gleamed, a crucifix stood. On the shoulders of a prelate was the purple that had dazzled the world.

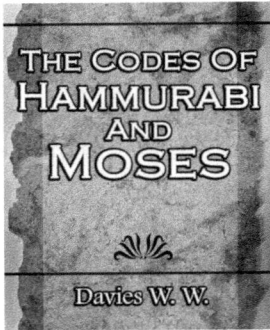

The Codes Of Hammurabi And Moses
W. W. Davies

The discovery of the Hammurabi Code is one of the greatest achievements of archaeology, and is of paramount interest, not only to the student of the Bible, but also to all those interested in ancient history...

Religion   **ISBN:** *1-59462-338-4*   **Pages:132**
MSRP $12.95   QTY

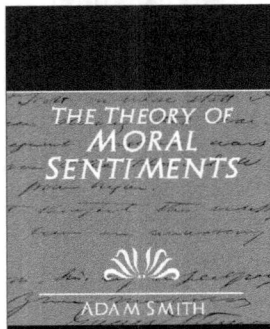

The Theory of Moral Sentiments
Adam Smith

This work from 1749. contains original theories of conscience amd moral judgment and it is the foundation for systemof morals.

Philosophy **ISBN:** *1-59462-777-0*   **Pages:536**
MSRP $19.95   QTY

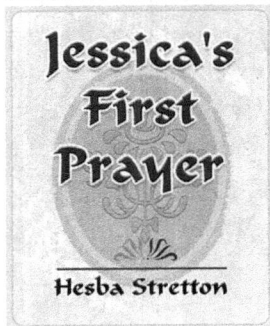

Jessica's First Prayer
Hesba Stretton

In a screened and secluded corner of one of the many railway-bridges which span the streets of London there could be seen a few years ago, from five o'clock every morning until half past eight, a tidily set-out coffee-stall, consisting of a trestle and board, upon which stood two large tin cans, with a small fire of charcoal burning under each so as to keep the coffee boiling during the early hours of the morning when the work-people were thronging into the city on their way to their daily toil...

Childrens   **ISBN:** *1-59462-373-2*   **Pages:84**
MSRP $9.95   QTY

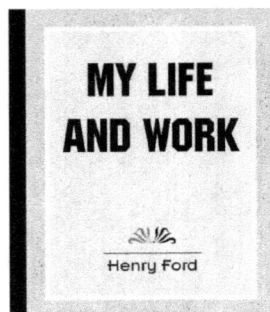

My Life and Work
Henry Ford

Henry Ford revolutionized the world with his implementation of mass production for the Model T automobile. Gain valuable business insight into his life and work with his own auto-biography... "We have only started on our development of our country we have not as yet, with all our talk of wonderful progress, done more than scratch the surface. The progress has been wonderful enough but..."

Biographies/   **ISBN:** *1-59462-198-5*   **Pages:300**
MSRP $21.95   QTY

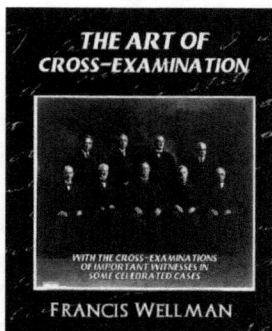

The Art of Cross-Examination
Francis Wellman

QTY

I presume it is the experience of every author, after his first book is published upon an important subject, to be almost overwhelmed with a wealth of ideas and illustrations which could readily have been included in his book, and which to his own mind, at least, seem to make a second edition inevitable. Such certainly was the case with me; and when the first edition had reached its sixth impression in five months, I rejoiced to learn that it seemed to my publishers that the book had met with a sufficiently favorable reception to justify a second and considerably enlarged edition. ..

Pages:412

Reference   ISBN: *1-59462-647-2*   *MSRP $19.95*

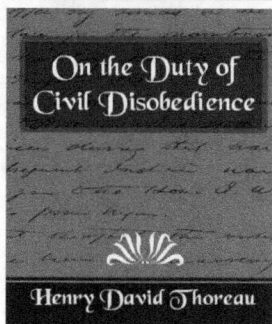

On the Duty of Civil Disobedience
Henry David Thoreau

QTY

Thoreau wrote his famous essay, On the Duty of Civil Disobedience, as a protest against an unjust but popular war and the immoral but popular institution of slave-owning. He did more than write—he declined to pay his taxes, and was hauled off to gaol in consequence. Who can say how much this refusal of his hastened the end of the war and of slavery ?

Law   ISBN: *1-59462-747-9*   **Pages:48**   *MSRP $7.45*

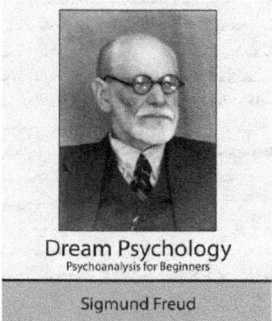

Dream Psychology Psychoanalysis for Beginners
Sigmund Freud

QTY

Sigmund Freud, born Sigismund Schlomo Freud (May 6, 1856 - September 23, 1939), was a Jewish-Austrian neurologist and psychiatrist who co-founded the psychoanalytic school of psychology. Freud is best known for his theories of the unconscious mind, especially involving the mechanism of repression; his redefinition of sexual desire as mobile and directed towards a wide variety of objects; and his therapeutic techniques, especially his understanding of transference in the therapeutic relationship and the presumed value of dreams as sources of insight into unconscious desires.

Pages:196

Psychology   ISBN: *1-59462-905-6*   *MSRP $15.45*

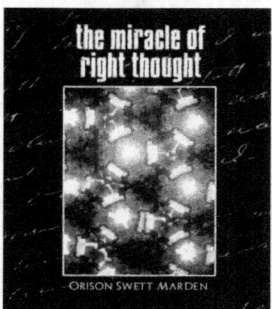

The Miracle of Right Thought
Orison Swett Marden

QTY

Believe with all of your heart that you will do what you were made to do. When the mind has once formed the habit of holding cheerful, happy, prosperous pictures, it will not be easy to form the opposite habit. It does not matter how improbable or how far away this realization may see, or how dark the prospects may be, if we visualize them as best we can, as vividly as possible, hold tenaciously to them and vigorously struggle to attain them, they will gradually become actualized, realized in the life. But a desire, a longing without endeavor, a yearning abandoned or held indifferently will vanish without realization.

Pages:360

Self Help   ISBN: *1-59462-644-8*   *MSRP $25.45*

The Rosicrucian Cosmo-Conception Mystic Christianity *by Max Heindel*   ISBN: *1-59462-188-8* **$38.95**
The Rosicrucian Cosmo-conception is not dogmatic, neither does it appeal to any other authority than the reason of the student. It is: not controversial, but is: sent forth in the, hope that it may help to clear...   New Age/Religion Pages 646

Abandonment To Divine Providence *by Jean-Pierre de Caussade*   ISBN: *1-59462-228-0* **$25.95**
"The Rev. Jean Pierre de Caussade was one of the most remarkable spiritual writers of the Society of Jesus in France in the 18th Century. His death took place at Toulouse in 1751. His works have gone through many editions and have been republished...   Inspirational/Religion Pages 400

Mental Chemistry *by Charles Haanel*   ISBN: *1-59462-192-6* **$23.95**
Mental Chemistry allows the change of material conditions by combining and appropriately utilizing the power of the mind. Much like applied chemistry creates something new and unique out of careful combinations of chemicals the mastery of mental chemistry...   New Age/Business Pages 354

The Letters of Robert Browning and Elizabeth Barret Barrett 1845-1846 vol II   ISBN: *1-59462-193-4* **$35.95**
by Robert Browning and Elizabeth Barrett   Biographies Pages 596

Gleanings In Genesis (volume I) *by Arthur W. Pink*   ISBN: *1-59462-130-6* **$27.45**
Appropriately has Genesis been termed "the seed plot of the Bible" for in it we have, in germ form, almost all of the great doctrines which are afterwards fully developed in the books of Scripture which follow...   Religion/Inspirational Pages 420

The Master Key *by L. W. de Laurence*   ISBN: *1-59462-001-6* **$30.95**
In no branch of human knowledge has there been a more lively increase of the spirit of research during the past few years than in the study of Psychology, Concentration and Mental Discipline. The requests for authentic lessons in Thought Control, Mental Discipline and...   New Age/Business Pages 422

The Lesser Key Of Solomon Goetia *by L. W. de Laurence*   ISBN: *1-59462-092-X* **$9.95**
This translation of the first book of the "Lernegton" which is now for the first time made accessible to students of Talismanic Magic was done, after careful collation and edition, from numerous Ancient Manuscripts in Hebrew, Latin, and French...   New Age/Occult Pages 92

Rubaiyat Of Omar Khayyam *by Edward Fitzgerald*   ISBN: *1-59462-332-5* **$13.95**
Edward Fitzgerald, whom the world has already learned, in spite of his own efforts to remain within the shadow of anonymity, to look upon as one of the rarest poets of the century, was born at Bredfield, in Suffolk, on the 31st of March, 1809. He was the third son of John Purcell...   Music Pages 172

Ancient Law *by Henry Maine*   ISBN: *1-59462-128-4* **$29.95**
The chief object of the following pages is to indicate some of the earliest ideas of mankind, as they are reflected in Ancient Law, and to point out the relation of those ideas to modern thought.   Religion/History Pages 452

Far-Away Stories *by William J. Locke*   ISBN: *1-59462-129-2* **$19.45**
"Good wine needs no bush, but a collection of mixed vintages does. And this book is just such a collection. Some of the stories I do not want to remain buried for ever in the museum files of dead magazine-numbers an author's not unpardonable vanity..."   Fiction Pages 272

Life of David Crockett *by David Crockett*   ISBN: *1-59462-250-7* **$27.45**
"Colonel David Crockett was one of the most remarkable men of the times in which he lived. Born in humble life, but gifted with a strong will, an indomitable courage, and unremitting perseverance...   Biographies/New Age Pages 424

Lip-Reading *by Edward Nitchie*   ISBN: *1-59462-206-X* **$25.95**
Edward B. Nitchie, founder of the New York School for the Hard of Hearing, now the Nitchie School of Lip-Reading, Inc, wrote "LIP-READING Principles and Practice". The development and perfecting of this meritorious work on lip-reading was an undertaking...   How-to Pages 400

A Handbook of Suggestive Therapeutics, Applied Hypnotism, Psychic Science   ISBN: *1-59462-214-0* **$24.95**
by Henry Munro   Health/New Age/Health/Self-help Pages 376

A Doll's House: and Two Other Plays *by Henrik Ibsen*   ISBN: *1-59462-112-8* **$19.95**
Henrik Ibsen created this classic when in revolutionary 1848 Rome. Introducing some striking concepts in playwriting for the realist genre, this play has been studied the world over.   Fiction/Classics/Plays 308

The Light of Asia *by sir Edwin Arnold*   ISBN: *1-59462-204-3* **$13.95**
In this poetic masterpiece, Edwin Arnold describes the life and teachings of Buddha. The man who was to become known as Buddha to the world was born as Prince Gautama of India but he rejected the worldly riches and abandoned the reigns of power when...   Religion/History/Biographies Pages 170

The Complete Works of Guy de Maupassant *by Guy de Maupassant*   ISBN: *1-59462-157-8* **$16.95**
"For days and days, nights and nights, I had dreamed of that first kiss which was to consecrate our engagement, and I knew not on what spot I should put my lips..."   Fiction/Classics Pages 240

The Art of Cross-Examination *by Francis L. Wellman*   ISBN: *1-59462-309-0* **$26.95**
Written by a renowned trial lawyer, Wellman imparts his experience and uses case studies to explain how to use psychology to extract desired information through questioning.   How-to/Science/Reference Pages 408

Answered or Unanswered? *by Louisa Vaughan*   ISBN: *1-59462-248-5* **$10.95**
Miracles of Faith in China   Religion Pages 112

The Edinburgh Lectures on Mental Science (1909) *by Thomas*   ISBN: *1-59462-008-3* **$11.95**
This book contains the substance of a course of lectures recently given by the writer in the Queen Street Hail, Edinburgh. Its purpose is to indicate the Natural Principles governing the relation between Mental Action and Material Conditions...   New Age/Psychology Pages 148

Ayesha *by H. Rider Haggard*   ISBN: *1-59462-301-5* **$24.95**
Verily and indeed it is the unexpected that happens! Probably if there was one person upon the earth from whom the Editor of this, and of a certain previous history, did not expect to hear again...   Classics Pages 380

Ayala's Angel *by Anthony Trollope*   ISBN: *1-59462-352-X* **$29.95**
The two girls were both pretty, but Lucy who was twenty-one who supposed to be simple and comparatively unattractive, whereas Ayala was credited, as her Bombwhat romantic name might show, with poetic charm and a taste for romance. Ayala when her father died was nineteen...   Fiction Pages 484

The American Commonwealth *by James Bryce*   ISBN: *1-59462-286-8* **$34.45**
An interpretation of American democratic political theory. It examines political mechanics and society from the perspective of Scotsman James Bryce   Politics Pages 572

Stories of the Pilgrims *by Margaret P. Pumphrey*   ISBN: *1-59462-116-0* **$17.95**
This book explores pilgrims religious oppression in England as well as their escape to Holland and eventual crossing to America on the Mayflower, and their early days in New England...   History Pages 268

www.bookjungle.com *email: sales@bookjungle.com fax: 630-214-0564 mail: Book Jungle PO Box 2226 Champaign, IL 61825*

QTY

The Fasting Cure *by Sinclair Upton*   ISBN: *1-59462-222-1* **$13.95**
In the Cosmopolitan Magazine for May, 1910, and in the Contemporary Review (London) for April, 1910, I published an article dealing with my experiences in fasting. I have written a great many magazine articles, but never one which attracted so much attention... New Age/Self Help/Health Pages 164

Hebrew Astrology *by Sepharial*   ISBN: *1-59462-308-2* **$13.45**
In these days of advanced thinking it is a matter of common observation that we have left many of the old landmarks behind and that we are now pressing forward to greater heights and to a wider horizon than that which represented the mind-content of our progenitors... Astrology Pages 144

Thought Vibration or The Law of Attraction in the Thought World   ISBN: *1-59462-127-6* **$12.95**
by William Walker Atkinson   *Psychology/Religion Pages 144*

Optimism *by Helen Keller*   ISBN: *1-59462-108-X* **$15.95**
Helen Keller was blind, deaf, and mute since 19 months old, yet famously learned how to overcome these handicaps, communicate with the world, and spread her lectures promoting optimism. An inspiring read for everyone... Biographies/Inspirational Pages 84

Sara Crewe *by Frances Burnett*   ISBN: *1-59462-360-0* **$9.45**
In the first place, Miss Minchin lived in London. Her home was a large, dull, tall one, in a large, dull square, where all the houses were alike, and all the sparrows were alike, and where all the door-knockers made the same heavy sound... Childrens/Classic Pages 88

The Autobiography of Benjamin Franklin *by Benjamin Franklin*   ISBN: *1-59462-135-7* **$24.95**
The Autobiography of Benjamin Franklin has probably been more extensively read than any other American historical work, and no other book of its kind has had such ups and downs of fortune. Franklin lived for many years in England, where he was agent... Biographies/History Pages 332

Name	
Email	
Telephone	
Address	
City, State ZIP	

☐ **Credit Card**   ☐ **Check / Money Order**

Credit Card Number	
Expiration Date	
Signature	

Please Mail to: Book Jungle
PO Box 2226
Champaign, IL 61825
or Fax to: 630-214-0564

ORDERING INFORMATION
web*: www.bookjungle.com*
email*: sales@bookjungle.com*
fax*: 630-214-0564*
mail*: Book Jungle PO Box 2226 Champaign, IL 61825*
or PayPal *to sales@bookjungle.com*

Please contact us for bulk discounts

DIRECT-ORDER TERMS

**20% Discount if You Order
Two or More Books**
Free Domestic Shipping!
Accepted: Master Card, Visa,
Discover, American Express